"We live in an increasingly open world, and in *The Open Organization: Igniting Passion and Performance,* Jim Whitehurst uses his experience in open source technology as a blueprint for leadership. Jim clearly demonstrates how building avidly engaged communities of employees, partners, and customers can ignite the kind of passion and innovation that drive outsized results for businesses and for society as a whole. This is a great read for anyone hoping to lead and succeed in a society being redefined by expectations of transparency, authenticity, access—and yes, in a word, openness."

—**MICHAEL DELL,** Chairman and CEO, Dell

"In a wired world, everyone knows that management needs to change from 'command and control' to leadership based on transparency, collaboration, and participation. But the question is, how do you actually lead that way? How does a leader give up so much power for something that looks like chaos? How do you get the leap in performance that comes from unleashing people's passion and creativity? Jim Whitehurst's interesting tale of his own reinvention as a leader, with lessons from other leaders in companies such as Whole Foods, Pixar, Zappos, and others, finally provides the blueprint that leaders have been seeking."

—**CHRIS ANDERSON,** cofounder and CEO, 3D Robotics; former
    Editor in Chief, *Wired* magazine

"Many people are wary of change. If it's out of one's control, highly visible, and potentially volatile, it has the makings of a nightmare. For executives who worry about Millennial employees and the power of the internet, it is scary indeed. Yet those same employees could offer valuable new perspectives, ideas, and passion. The question is, how do today's managers capture those desirable attributes without setting off the perfect storm? The answers are in Jim Whitehurst's book *The Open Organization: Igniting Passion and Performance.*"

—**JEANIE DANIEL DUCK,** former Senior Partner and Managing Director, The Boston Consulting Group; author, *The Change Monster*

"In today's disruptive economy, only the leaders—and their organizations—who are open and learn to adapt to the fast-changing needs of customers and employees will survive. Whitehurst speaks from personal experience about what works—and what doesn't—to foster openness and speed. If you have even an inkling of a desire to lead an innovative, fast-moving, and engaged organization, this book is for you."

—**CHARLENE LI,** founder and CEO, Altimeter Group; author, *The Engaged Leader* and *Open Leadership*

"Drawing from the lessons he's learned leading an organization born directly from the principles of open source, Jim Whitehurst offers us an invaluable guide to success for the modern organization based on true openness, collaboration, and shared commitment. With *The Open Organization*, Whitehurst takes us where all leaders need to be if we want to succeed in the future—outside of our traditional comfort zones."

—**JOHN CHAMBERS,** Chairman and CEO, Cisco

THE OPEN

ORGANIZATION

THE OPEN

ORGANIZATION

IGNITING PASSION AND PERFORMANCE

JIM WHITEHURST

CEO, RED HAT

with a Foreword by GARY HAMEL

HARVARD BUSINESS REVIEW PRESS
BOSTON, MASSACHUSETTS

Copyright 2015 Red Hat, Inc.
All rights reserved
Printed in the United States of America

10 9 8 7 6 5 4 3 2 1

No part of this publication may be reproduced, stored in or introduced into a retrieval system, or transmitted, in any form, or by any means (electronic, mechanical, photocopying, recording, or otherwise), without the prior permission of the publisher. Requests for permission should be directed to permissions@hbsp.harvard.edu, or mailed to Permissions, Harvard Business School Publishing, 60 Harvard Way, Boston, Massachusetts 02163.

The web addresses referenced in this book were live and correct at the time of the book's publication but may be subject to change.

Library of Congress Cataloging-in-Publication Data

Whitehurst, Jim.
  The open organization : igniting passion and performance / Jim Whitehurst.
    pages cm
  ISBN 978-1-62527-527-1 (hardback)
1. Organizational effectiveness. 2. Organizational behavior. 3. Organizational change. 4. Employee motivation. 5. Management—Employee participation. 6. Decentralization in management. I. Title.
HD58.9.W526 2015
658.3'152—dc23

2014045002

The paper used in this publication meets the requirements of the American National Standard for Permanence of Paper for Publications and Documents in Libraries and Archives Z39.48-1992.

This book is dedicated to the millions of
open source contributors and users out there
who make what we do possible.

CONTENTS

PART THREE

WHAT
Setting Direction

FOREWORD

Here's a conundrum. The human capabilities that are most critical to success—the ones that can help your organization become more resilient, more creative, and more, well, awesome—are precisely the ones that can't be "managed." While you can compel financially dependent employees to be obedient and diligent, and can recruit the most intellectually capable, you can't command initiative, creativity, or passion. These human capabilities are, quite literally, gifts. Every day employees choose whether to bring them to work or leave them at home. Suppliers and customers make similar decisions—to engage with your enterprise in a spirit of true collaboration or apply their energies elsewhere. As a leader, how do you create an environment that inspires people to volunteer those "gifts"?

Nearly fifty years ago, Warren Bennis, the much-missed leadership guru, predicted that we'd soon be working in "organic-adaptive structures," organizations that feel like communities, not hierarchies. In a community, the basis for loyalty is a common purpose, not economic dependency. Control comes from shared norms and aspirations, not from policies and bosses. Rewards are mostly intrinsic rather than extrinsic. Contributions aren't predetermined and individuals are free to contribute as they may. Examples are as diverse as a meeting of Alcoholics Anonymous or a team erecting a house for Habitat for Humanity.

Bennis had a compelling vision, but until recently it was hard to believe that community-centric structures could ever scale. Then came the internet. The defining characteristic of the internet is its openness. Online, human beings are free to connect, contribute, and create as never before, and billions of them have exploited that opportunity. Consider YouTube. Every minute, more than a hundred hours of content are posted to YouTube, and each month, more than 6 billion hours of video are consumed by viewers from around the world. YouTube is open; anyone can contribute, and at present, more than a million contributors make money from content they've uploaded to the site.

I'm old enough to remember when networks were closed. Thirty years ago, if you wanted to add another telephone to your home, you leased it from the network operator—be it AT&T, BT, Bell Canada, or any other telco. Moreover, your phone was a dumb device. All the intelligence resided in the giant computers that routed your calls. To add a new service, like call-waiting, the operator had to reprogram the central switch, an expensive and risky endeavor. Screw it up and you could bring down the whole network. Not surprisingly, innovation proceeded at a snail's pace. Today, the web hosts hundreds of web-based communication services including Apple's iMessage, WhatsApp, Snapchat, Kakao Talk, Google Hangout, WeChat, and Grasshopper. On Skype alone, users spend more than 2 billion minutes communicating each day.

The web has also spawned thousands of special interest groups, like wrongplanet.net, a site dedicated to improving the lives of individuals with autism. The community's eighty thousand members have posted more than 1.2 million comments on the site's general discussion board. In many important respects, the web is a community of communities.

Unlike your organization, the web's architecture is end-to-end rather than center-to-end. That's what makes it adaptable, captivating, and a platform for innovation. Not surprisingly, many have been bullish about the opportunity to replace bureaucracy with web-style collaboration. Thus far, though, the reality hasn't matched the hype.

A wiki can surface new options, but it can't manage a global product launch. A "smart mob" can oust a dictator, but it can't organize itself to collect the garbage and keep the trains running. The wisdom of the crowd can predict elections, but it can't run the back office of a bank. YouTube may be a mind-boggling jumble of content, but operationally it's run by Google—the same company that delivers your search results in a nanosecond. Bureaucracy was invented to maximize control, coordination, and consistency—things that are essential to reliability and efficiency but aren't the hallmarks of online communities and open innovation projects.

So are we stuck? On one hand, we have all those optimistic boosters for social collaboration who tell us we merely have to let the crowd have its say. That's naive. What's typically underestimated is the complexity and indivisibility of many large-scale coordination tasks. "Wisdom of the crowd" works when work can be easily disaggregated and individuals can work in relative isolation. That's why it's been so well suited to software development. But it's not easy to see how you'd use it to run a Toyota automotive plant or Delta's Atlanta maintenance facility. Despite the buzz, the limits of crowdsourcing and open innovation have relegated them to the margins of most organizations.

What about the other hand? There you'll find thousands of executives who can scarcely imagine an alternative to the organizational status quo, even if they believe that their bureaucratic organizations are gunking up the wheels of progress and diminishing their ability to play against faster, more nimble competitors. Because it's what they've learned and have succeeded at, they hold on to top-down, rule-driven structures that empower the few while disempowering the many. And it's because they've never seen something like General Electric's jet engine plant in Durham, North Carolina, where four hundred skilled technicians work in self-organizing teams with but a single plant manager to supervise them. They've never been inside a company like Morning Star, the world's largest tomato processor, where hundreds of colleagues coordinate their activities via peer-to-peer agreements, with nary a boss in sight. Neither have they been up close with CEMEX, the Mexico-based cement company that uses hundreds of online, user-defined communities to build brands, share best practices, and create strategy.

So no, we're not stuck; we're *definitely* not stuck. But getting unstuck—building and benefiting from communities at scale—requires us to start with "openness" as a principle, rather than with some particular set of collaborative tools or practices. Many companies have layered social technologies on top of their tradition-encrusted management practices—and most have been disappointed with the results. Such superficial gestures can never change an organization. To fully exploit the power of openness, we have to go much, much deeper. We have to get at the ethos of openness, and then see how it applies, in practice, in hiring employees, making decisions, running operations, allocating resources, and all of the other things that, surprisingly enough, communities can do better than bureaucrats.

And that's exactly what Jim Whitehurst, CEO of Red Hat, does in this practical and compelling book. Red Hat, with its seven thousand associates, is one of a small but growing number of companies that have transcended the old trade-offs between scale and agility, efficiency and innovation, and discipline and empowerment. In the pages that follow, Jim shows you how to operationalize the ideas of transparency, collegiality, and meritocracy in *your* organization. More importantly, he challenges you to rethink your most fundamental assumptions about how you get things done—not little, marginal things, but big, complicated, mission-critical things.

I have long believed that tomorrow's most successful organizations will be distinguished by a set of traits that are still remarkably uncommon. In organizations that are fit for the future . . .

- Leaders will be chosen by the led.

- Contribution will matter more than credentials.

- Influence will come from your value added, not your title.

- Individuals will compete to make a difference, not to climb a pyramid.

- Compensation will be set by peers, not bosses.

- Every idea will compete on an equal footing.

- Resources will be allocated with market-like mechanisms.

- Experimentation and fast prototyping will be core competencies.

- Communities of passion will be the basic organizational building blocks.

- Coordination will occur through collaboration, not centralization.

- Lateral communication will be more important than vertical communication.

- Structure will emerge only where it creates value and disappear everywhere else.

- Strategy making will be a dynamic, companywide conversation.

- Change will start in unexpected places and get rolled up, not out.

- Control will be achieved through transparency and peer feedback.

- Organizational boundaries will be porous.

- Everyone will think like a business owner, and be just as accountable.

- Decisions will be made as close to the coal face as possible.

- Commitments will be voluntary.

- "Why" will matter more than "what."

What makes Jim's book so timely is that Red Hat already embodies many of these postbureaucratic traits, so there is a ton you can learn here—not only from Red Hat, but from the other organizations Jim draws on in building his case for the "open organization."

Let me finish where I started. Today, most organizations waste more human capacity than they use. How much longer do you think your organization will be able to afford that, given that more and more companies are embracing the principles that power Red Hat? My answer? Not as long as you think. So what are you waiting for? Dig in.

Gary Hamel
Visiting Professor, London Business School

1

Why Opening Up
Your Organization
Matters

Whenever I talk with leaders of companies in industries from manufacturing to retail, from software to consumer goods, I hear a consistent theme: frustration that they can't move fast enough, given the organizations they have, to stay competitive. They know that capabilities like speed and agility are becoming the core of competitive advantage, and yet most of them struggle to keep their organizations moving as rapidly as all the changes in their environments. The typical chain of command is too slow to respond to opportunities. Central planning takes too long and consumes too many resources. Internal resources alone are too limited to address the challenges of today, let alone tomorrow.

To succeed, these leaders know they must build organizations capable of successfully navigating the challenges of a fast-paced environment, but they don't know where to start. That's because the classic rules of the game—which used to define who won or lost in business—are being swept away. Old standby strategies that everyone learned in business school—like scale, scarcity, and positional advantage—no longer seem to apply. Continuing to do what they've done before—and just pedaling harder—doesn't seem to work anymore. What is the new organizational model for success? And how do you build it?

If you lead or aspire to lead an organization of any kind, then you face these same challenges. You can't keep doing things the way you've always done them. You need to tap the knowledge, creativity, ideas, energy, and power of your employees. At the same time, you know that needed talent, ideas, and resources lie outside your company—and that your organization's success depends on successfully tapping into those sources of knowledge, too. That means you must further knock down the walls of your organization in ways that allow you to collaborate with your customers, vendors, and partners—to open up your organization in a way that keeps you on the cutting edge of change.

An "open organization"—which I define as an organization that engages participative communities both inside and out—responds to opportunities more quickly, has access to resources and talent outside the organization, and inspires, motivates, and empowers people at all levels to act with accountability. The beauty of an open organization is that it is not about pedaling harder, but about tapping into new sources of power both inside and outside to keep pace with all the fast-moving changes in your environment.

But how do you make this kind of organizational model work? How do you harness the power of the crowd *inside* (your employees) as well as *outside* (everyone else)—especially at scale?

This book reveals the secrets of how an open organization really works by taking an insider's in-depth look into one of the premier open organizations in the world, Red Hat (a software company with a value of more than $10 billion where I am the CEO), along with illustrative examples of other companies operating this way too, such as Whole Foods, Pixar, Zappos, Starbucks, W. L. Gore, and others. This book will show leaders and aspiring leaders—in companies large and small, and in established companies as well as start-ups struggling to grow—how to develop a new, open organizational model that uniquely matches the speed and complexity that businesses must master today.

From Crowdsourcing to Open Sourcing

Much has been written recently about a new way of working called "crowdsourcing," which is the power of mass participation to generate phenomenal ideas, solve complex problems, and organize broad movements. We've seen examples, such as Wikipedia or the Linux operating system (which played a key role in Red Hat's start), where communities of people spontaneously self-organize around a problem or activity. Work is distributed in a network-like fashion and people are held accountable, all without a formal hierarchy. A growing number of organizations have learned to successfully tap the "wisdom of the crowd" (as documented by James Surowiecki in his book of the same name) in order to drive innovation and gain a competitive advantage through collaboration. The power of these networks has been well documented and explored in books like *Wikinomics* and *Macrowikinomics* by Don Tapscott and Anthony D. Williams; Clay Shirky's *Here Comes Everybody*; *Crowdsourcing* by Jeff Howe; and the numerous books and articles by open innovation evangelist Henry Chesbrough.

Many big-name companies, ranging from General Electric and Dell to IBM and Starbucks, have turned to the crowd as a way to generate new product ideas and turn customer feedback into the seeds of innovation. Consumer product giant Procter & Gamble does all that and more; it has developed a program through which it collaborates with smaller entrepreneurial companies to bring new game-changing products to market. In the program's first two years alone, it reportedly generated two thousand new ideas, one hundred of which were turned into new product lines. Or consider Threadless.com, a company that uses its community of consumers and artists to make and sell clever T-shirts, both through its own site and more recently through a partnership with The Gap. There's even a company called InnoCentive that firms can hire to help them use the power of the crowd.

There are also competitions like the Ansari XPRIZE, which awarded $10 million to the first nongovernment organization to launch a reusable manned spacecraft into space twice within two weeks, or Kaggle, which crowdsources solutions to big data–type analytical challenges, that get a multitude of participants to deliver a bunch of ideas or solutions, where the single best of the bunch wins and receives an award.

The Limitations of Crowdsourcing

As effective as these "tapping the wisdom of the crowd" approaches are at providing companies with new ideas and solutions to problems, they are often limited in that they are either timebound, say, for the duration of a competition, or are narrowly focused on a single, specific goal, such as generating an idea for a new product. It's a one-and-done kind of result and not the basis for any kind of sustainable competitive advantage. So, while many companies have tapped the power of participation in targeted ways, few have leveraged its power more broadly within their own organizations. *What if you could make this kind of engagement standard, not just one-and-done, for how work gets done in your organization, so that you're engaging at this level every single day?*

Another problem with crowdsourcing is that it's a one-way transaction. Crowdsourcing approaches typically depend on the contributions of volunteers—people who contribute to the product primarily for the reputational advantage, not necessarily for a monetary one. And, too often, it seems that companies approach these volunteers with the goal of extracting value, with what has been called a "Tom Sawyer" model of collaboration.[1] As you might recall from your childhood reading, Tom was a bit of a manipulator, someone who was always trying to get out of doing chores. One time in particular, he was tasked with whitewashing his Aunt Polly's fence as a punishment. So Tom reached out to his community and tricked his friends into doing the work for him by pretending that it was a whole lot of fun to do the job. He even got them to exchange trinkets for the privilege of doing the work.

While this approach worked for Tom once, it certainly wouldn't happen again. Similarly, when today's organizations reach out to the crowd—both inside and outside their walls—they're thinking the way Tom Sawyer did by asking for help without giving much in return. This is rarely sustainable. *What if there were a way to treat both those outside your company and those within your company differently, in a way that truly inspires, motivates, and rewards top performance?*

The Promise of Open Source

One model that successfully harnesses the power and commitment of talent and engages that talent in an ongoing way over time is open source. The term "open source" is traditionally used in the software arena and designates a process in which anyone can contribute to or access code, unlike traditional software development, which is proprietary and owned by the company that produces it and governed by intellectual property law. In open source, those who do the work volunteer their time and effort, and these volunteer, participative communities are both long running and capable of tackling multiple problems and opportunities simultaneously.

For examples of open source communities, think about the phenomenal innovations that continue to come out of Silicon Valley—far more than any one company could generate on its own—or how scientists worldwide worked together to unravel the human genome. The US legal system is another great example of the innovative power of an open community. Can you imagine any single person or even team of lawyers sitting down to create a set of rules vast and flexible enough to encapsulate a legal system that has, in fact, grown organically on a case-by-case basis? It's an extraordinarily complex system in which attorneys' individual arguments and judges' opinions ripple out and have an impact on the lives of millions of people. And it's a system that depends on the deep engagement of many diverse individuals playing different roles, building on the work of each other, in this case, over centuries.

Open source communities operate on a level beyond crowdsourcing, going beyond the one-way and one-time-only arrangements in which a lot of people give their ideas or answers but don't engage with each other over time. Instead, the way they operate is better described as *open sourcing*, where contributors work together as a community, building on each other's work, to arrive at the best solution to a complicated problem. These communities involve many people working toward a similar outcome. They usually involve a diverse community of people who opt in as a way to work for a common cause about which they are passionate. And they produce results: they are more responsive to fast-changing environments and better at accomplishing "big, hairy, audacious goals" than any one single firm or organization.[2]

Now imagine the impact of applying that kind of power within your own business, where talent from a diverse range of organizations and backgrounds—external volunteers from the crowd as well as your own employees and in-house teams—all come together to work toward something your customers can benefit from. But can a single organization catalyze or influence disparate groups on its own? How do you get people fired up and passionate about volunteering their efforts, whether they are outside or inside the organization, toward something your organization will gain from?

Clearly, it's not enough to just employ the strategy of "build it and they will come." They won't. Or if they do, without a set of guidelines in place, you could wind up generating more ill will than value by asking for help. Asking people to contribute their time and energy can be the competitive edge that propels an organization forward—or an anchor that pulls it down.

But when it's done well—wow! Imagine how innovative and responsive your organization would be if it could constantly generate new ideas and deliver on them without any top-down interference? That's the promise of open sourcing.

To do this, you must transition into thinking of people as members of a community, moving from a transactional mind-set to one built on commitment. Perhaps more importantly, you need to apply the same principles to your employees—the folks you pay—as to people who might volunteer their efforts for free. Just because someone is on your payroll doesn't ensure that you are getting the best of his or her abilities. Or that another organization won't lure your superstars away. You need something more to hook them in a way that inspires them to truly opt in and bring their passion and energy to their work every day. What you need, in short, is to build a culture that truly embraces the notion of being *open* in every sense of that word. When you can accomplish that, the results are astounding.

This book explains how to lead and manage the open way.

The Open Organization

One company that not only gets the idea of open source, but was born out of the open source movement, is Red Hat, the world's leading provider of open source software solutions. It's perhaps no surprise that a company that has built a business running and operating open source systems—where openness, transparency, participation, and collaboration are the very basis for how the company makes money—espouses those same principles when managing it. Red Hat has been managed using open source principles for more than twenty years. Managing and leading an open organization could not be more different from leading a more conventional one.

I know because I'm the company's president and chief executive officer. Red Hat was an open organization long before I ever came on board in 2007. Long before I joined Red Hat, I made my mark as a quintessential top-down kind of leader. This company changed me and taught me how to be a better leader; this book is largely about the lessons I've learned on why an open organization is so much better than a traditional one, and how to lead one.

Red Hat's Success

Red Hat is recognized for reliability, profitability, and growth: its stock is publicly traded with a market value of more than $10 billion.

One of very few software companies with annual revenues of nearly $2 billion and certainly the only open source one, it's been lauded by publications like *Forbes*, *Bloomberg Businessweek*, and others for cutting-edge innovation and for being a great place to work.[3] It's part of the Standard & Poor's 500 and has more than seven thousand associates. You may not have heard of Red Hat, but you're likely using its technology every day. Its products power airline systems, banking networks, and underlie the majority of stock market equity trades. It counts more than 90 percent of the *Fortune* 500 as customers, as well as influential organizations such as DreamWorks, Sprint, and the New York Stock Exchange.

Its success comes from the open organization model.

A New Management Paradigm

Red Hat's open organization operates using unusual management principles that leverage the power of participation—both internally and externally—to generate consistent financial results. It uses open sourcing to tap a massive, disparate community of people, all with different skills and motivations, to make super-high-performing products capable of running some of the most secure and mission-critical computer systems in the world. We've learned that to successfully reap the rewards from open sourcing something, we have to engage and support the community as we work together on shared goals. We don't just look to a crowd for ideas. We innovate in, with, and through communities. By embracing participation from contributors within and outside the walls of the organization, Red Hat has created a competitive advantage that enables it to compete against—and beat—far larger rivals. Red Hat operates in a really fast-paced environment, and the organizational structure, an open one, is the best way for it to keep pace with the flurry of changes it faces every single day. We have harnessed the power of what economists call the "network effect" that results when you connect people and ideas. The more people you connect, the more value they create, which in turn attracts more people, and so on. Red Hat's management system encompasses principles such as:

- People join us because they want to.

- Contribution is critical, but it's not a quid pro quo.

- The best ideas win regardless of who they come from.

- We encourage and expect open, frank, and passionate debate.

- We welcome feedback and make changes in the spirit of "release early—release often."

In short, we've found that the best practices in creating open source software also translate well into managing the entire company.

We have leveraged these components to create a new sort of company—an open organization—a rebooted, redesigned, reinvented organization suitable for the decentralized, empowered digital age. By opening up the business and encouraging participation at every level, from both within and outside the organization, we've obtained the incredible results I've described.

Red Hat is the only company that can say it emerged out of a pure bottom-up culture—namely, the open source ethos—and learned how to execute it at scale. It has gone beyond the theories and developed a leadership system that works, one that everyone from CEOs to departmental managers and aspiring leaders need to pay attention to because it emerged specifically to address the new rules of business and a socially connected and conscious workforce. Red Hat is the epicenter for a new management paradigm. The purpose of this book is to show you how to create this kind of open, community-driven culture and how to lead it in a way that allows your organization to get more done, faster, and with more innovative results.

Leading the Open Organization

Before I arrived at Red Hat, I had spent most of my professional career devoted to studying businesses. As a partner with The Boston Consulting Group (BCG), where I worked for ten years (with a two-year stint attending Harvard Business School), I saw the inner workings of literally hundreds of companies. My job was simple: identify and solve problems. I was there to help companies recognize their limitations and figure out ways to overcome them. Similarly, as chief operating officer at Delta Air Lines, I was chief problem solver and took a lead role in Delta's restructuring. I learned a lot over my six years there, as well as during my time at BCG. I thought I knew how well-performing organizations should operate. I thought I knew what it took to manage people and get work done. But the techniques I had learned, the traditional beliefs I held for management and how people are taught to run companies and lead organizations, were to be challenged when I entered the world of Red Hat and open source.

Red Hat has shown me alternatives to the traditional approach to leadership and management—ones better suited to the fast-paced environment of business. The conventional approach to business management was not designed to foster innovation, address the needs and expectations of the current workforce that demands more of jobs (hello, Millennials), or operate at the accelerated speed of business. I came to realize, in other words, that the conventional way of running companies had major limitations that are now becoming more acute.

My change in thinking began in 2007. I had just left Delta after helping the company through a successful turnaround. A new CEO had come in and I felt it was the right time for me to move on and find my next opportunity. Because Delta was such a high-profile company and the turnaround was considered successful, I received dozens of calls from recruiters offering opportunities—especially more chances to turn around companies—at a wide variety of companies, from private equity firms to *Fortune* 500 giants. I'll admit that, after years of hard work, it was nice to be wined and dined and courted by such big names.

Then I received a call from a recruiter for Red Hat. Being somewhat of a computer person myself—my undergraduate degree at Rice University was in computer science—I knew about Red Hat's core Linux product and had been using the desktop version for some time. But I didn't know much about the company itself or the true extent of how pervasive open source development had become. After doing some research, I was intrigued. Part of the appeal came from the fact that I was wary of taking on any other turnaround opportunities after my time at Delta. I had been in charge of laying off tens of thousands of people. As someone who cared deeply about the people with whom I worked, I found the process extremely painful for my associates and myself. Many of the other companies courting me wanted more of the same. I just couldn't do it. I hated laying people off. Red Hat, on the other hand, offered something very different. It was growing. It offered me a chance to help create something new while also getting back to my tech roots. I found it extraordinary how a company could make so much money selling software that, in theory, anyone could download off the internet for free.[4]

After telling the recruiter I was interested in the interview, he asked if I would mind flying to Red Hat's headquarters in Raleigh, North Carolina, on a Sunday. I thought to myself that Sunday was a strange day to schedule a meeting. But I was headed up to New York on Monday anyway, so I could stop on the way, and I agreed to the interview. I hopped a plane from Atlanta to the Raleigh-Durham airport. My cab dropped me off in front of the Red Hat building, then on the campus of North Carolina State University. It was 9:30 a.m. on Sunday, and there was no one in sight. The lights were off, and, after a check, I found the doors were locked. Was this a gag? I wondered. As I turned to get back in the cab, I noticed the driver had already pulled away. Just about that same time, it started raining. I had no umbrella.

As I started to walk somewhere to hail a cab, Matthew Szulik, then Red Hat's chairman and CEO, rolled up in his car. "Hi there," he said. "Want to go grab some coffee?" While this seemed like a strange start to an interview, I knew I could certainly use some coffee. At the very least, I figured I'd be closer to getting a cab back to the airport.

In North Carolina, Sunday mornings are pretty quiet. It took us a while to even find a coffee shop that was open before noon. The shop wasn't the best in town or the cleanest, but it was open and had freshly brewed coffee. We grabbed a booth and began to chat.

After thirty minutes or so, I was feeling good about the way things were going. The interview wasn't traditional, but the conversation was great. Rather than dig into the nuts and bolts of Red Hat's corporate strategy or its image on Wall Street—things I had done homework on—Szulik asked me more about my hopes, dreams, and aspirations. It seems clear to me now that Szulik was gauging whether I was going to be a good fit for Red Hat's unique culture and management style.

After we finished, Szulik mentioned he wanted me to meet Michael Cunningham, the company's general counsel, and suggested maybe that I could have an early lunch with him. I agreed, so we started to get up to leave. As he grabbed for his wallet, Szulik realized he didn't have it. "Oops," he said. "I don't have any money. Do you?" This kind of caught me off guard, but I told him I had some money and didn't mind springing for the coffee.

A few minutes later, Szulik dropped me off at a little Mexican eatery where I met up with Cunningham. Again, this was not a traditional interview or setting by any means, but another great conversation. As Cunningham and I were getting ready to settle the bill, we were informed that the restaurant's credit card machine was broken. They could only take cash. Cunningham turned to me and asked if I could cover it because he had no cash. Since I was on my way to New York City, I had a good amount of cash so I paid for lunch.

Cunningham offered to give me a lift to the airport and we headed off in his car. Within minutes, he asked, "Do you mind if I stop and get some gas? We're running on fumes." "No problem," I replied. As soon as I heard the rhythmic thump of the pump begin, there was a tapping on my window. It was Cunningham. "Hey, they don't take credit cards here," he said. "Could I borrow some cash?" I was starting to wonder whether this was really an interview or some kind of scam.

While in New York the next day, I was talking to my wife about the interview with Red Hat. I told her the conversation had been great, but I wasn't sure whether they were serious about hiring me or if they just wanted some free food and gas. When I look back at that meeting now, I realize that Szulik and Cunningham were just being open and treating me like any other person they may have had coffee or lunch with or got gas with. Yes, it was ironic and funny that they both had no cash. But, for them, it wasn't about the money. They, like the open source world, didn't believe in rolling out red carpets for anyone or trying to make sure everything was perfect. They just wanted to get to know *me* rather than try to impress or court me. They wanted to know who I was.

That first interview with Red Hat showed me that working here would be different. There wasn't a traditional hierarchy and special treatment for leaders, at least not the kind that you might find at most other companies. In time, I also learned that Red Hat believed in the open source principle of meritocracy; that the best idea wins regardless of whether the idea comes from the top executive or a summer intern. Put another way, my early experiences with Red Hat introduced me to what the future of leadership looks like.

How I Learned to Lead the Open Organization

You can't lead an open organization in the traditional top-down fashion—what I was used to and, frankly, quite good at. I learned this the hard way.

My first instinct when I took the job was to recoil at what felt like chaos. "I need to get this company ordered and structured so that it performs better," I thought to myself. Over time, though, I've come to appreciate that Red Hat is the product of a complex, subtle, and powerful organizing system that truly frees people to be more creative, take initiative, and get more stuff done. Working here is inspiring and motivating, and it results in things getting done quickly. As a direct result, I've learned to change my own style of leadership to fit in rather than the other way around.

When I was at Delta, for example, I was incredibly detail oriented. I would receive daily fifteen-page reports, in the smallest font you can imagine, that would contain everything from yields per route to flight performance by airport and by fleet. In meetings I would ask why the Cincinnati–St. Louis route was underperforming and call out individuals if their numbers weren't up to par. I thought that leading meant making sure people were executing and holding them accountable for metrics. Eventually, I became known as the guy with the "binders" because of all that data I carried around with me.

My job at Red Hat couldn't be more different. Sure, I still care about numbers—we are a public company after all—but I have an impact on them indirectly by working through our people and culture. I spend the majority of my time thinking about our strategic direction and culture and talking to customers rather than worrying if things are being done precisely as I would choose. A huge part of that means trusting other people to do the right thing—to be hands-off enough to allow the people in the organization to direct themselves and make their own decisions.

That might sound a bit crazy to many, especially those who came up through conventionally run organizations as I did. I've written this book to help convince you that there is, in fact, a better way to run a company—an open and collaborative way. But, one thing I can personally vouch for is that shifting your mind-set isn't always easy. I thought by joining Red Hat I could change the company and help it grow up. After all, why had it hired me if not to change things in some way? But the truth is that Red Hat quickly changed me, especially my views on how companies can and should be run. Given today's realities, Red Hat has taught me that there is a better way.

I've also learned that the skills required to lead a company that relies heavily on the principles of open innovation are vastly different from those needed to run a business based on the hierarchical structure of a conventional organization. Changing the way you might be used to leading will be painful, but it will also be critical for every twenty-first century leader to understand and embrace.

Top-down decision making simply doesn't work at a company like Red Hat whose business model depends on collaboration and shared ideas, rather than control of assets. A person with positional authority can try to impose this kind of command-and-control model—after all, conventional organizations have been run that way for generations—but we've come to learn that it simply won't work here at Red Hat. Our people expect—actually, they demand—to have a voice in how we run the company, ranging from the mission statement to the travel policy. As CEO, I can't simply send orders down the ranks and expect everyone to jump on board. In order to drive engagement and collaboration to the roots of an organization, you need to get people involved in the decision-making process. And you know what? It works. Red Hat is a faster, leaner, and more innovative company as a result.

At Delta, for example, I led a massive organization of men and women who grew up in a world of hierarchy and who reliably followed the chain of command. So I was surprised to realize that at Red Hat, I had to build credibility and influence with the whole team before I could truly make an impact. Early on, I issued what I thought was an order to create a research report. A few days later, I asked the people assigned to the task how things were going. "Oh, we decided it was a bad idea, so we scrapped it," they told me in good cheer.

That's a difficult concept for many of my peers in other companies to embrace. Other CEOs to whom I've told this story have gasped, "What do you mean they didn't do what you asked them to? That's insubordination! You should have fired them." At first, I felt that way, too. But, the truth is that my team was right to turn down the job—it either wasn't a great idea or, just as importantly, I hadn't done a good enough job selling them on why they should jump into it. A leader's effectiveness is no longer measured by his or her ability to simply issue orders.

People need a thick skin to deal with the extensive and often relentless feedback involved in working the way we do at Red Hat.

It takes time, effort, and a good dose of humility—especially if you're the CEO—in order to build such a culture. (If you don't openly allow and encourage your employees to tell you you're wrong, you'll never build an organization that can innovate better than your competitors.) That means, of course, that we operate on the bleeding edge, as we continue to move forward, making plenty of mistakes and learning from them as we go.

My job is not about conjuring up brilliant strategies and making people work harder. What I need to do is create the context for Red Hat associates so they can do their best work. My goal is to get people to believe in the mission and then create the right structures that empower them to achieve what once might have been impossible.

It's a bit like living in the Old West. We have the opportunity to do something new. While that's exciting, it's also unsettling to think that everything you learned in business school or in running a conventional organization may be outdated or obsolete. Managing this kind of structure introduces a great deal of complexity and often makes decision making far harder. But the end result is nothing short of magic, something that Red Hat's shareholders, who have seen a quadrupling in the value of their stock over the past four years, can attest to.

What You Will Get from This Book

As word has leaked out about Red Hat's success and the collaborative nature of its culture, bellwether organizations like GE have asked, "How do you create such magic?" This book is the answer to that question. The principles, insights, and tips throughout will help you turn your organization into a more open one and will help you transform your own leadership style, as I've transformed mine.

But the lessons don't apply to just big companies. For too long, entre-preneurs have been told that eventually their organizations need to mature by embracing the conventional hierarchical systems that big companies use. The open organization offers an alternative to that kind of stale thinking. Small companies have much to gain by keep-ing the same participatory dynamics on which they now thrive to grow into the future.

Organizations of all shapes and sizes and in all kinds of industries can benefit from the open organization model in this book. Though I feature my own lessons as CEO of Red Hat and the voices of other Red Hat associates throughout, I'll also describe how companies such as Whole Foods, Pixar, Zappos, Starbucks, W. L. Gore, and others are applying and succeeding with these ideas, too.

Your New Playbook for Leading and Managing

In the following pages, I'll show you how to rewrite the rules for get-ting work done by tapping the power of the crowd inside and outside your organization's walls.

I will describe how an *open organization* management system—visually depicted in figure 1-1—functions differently from con-ventional management thinking in core areas like motivating and inspiring people, getting things done day-to-day, and setting direc-tion. The book is organized into six key areas in three sections—the *why*, the *how*, and the *what*—and describes how we as a team run the company based on the best practices we've culled from build-ing open source software. Some of these concepts will be familiar to readers; others will open up new areas of discussion. But the key point is that all these components complement each other and func-tion together as a cutting-edge management system that is the foun-dation for building participative communities. This is a blueprint for

FIGURE 1-1

The conventional organization versus the open organization

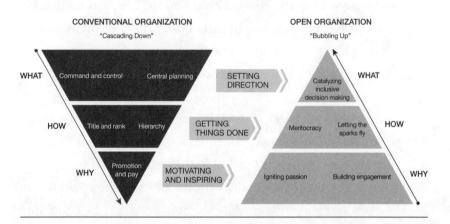

the kind of environment you as a leader need to create in order to get people to opt in to your community.

I'll focus on best practices, such as how to stoke employees' passion (chapter 2), how to engage the workforce (chapter 3), and why everyone in an open organization like Red Hat, including the CEO, has to earn a level of influence through merit (chapter 4). I'll also talk about how opening yourself up means that you need to find ways to encourage collaboration (chapter 5) and how decision making is a lengthy process, but once it is done, execution becomes much more effective (chapter 6). I'll wrap up by talking about the changing nature of leadership within a community (chapter 7) before discussing in the epilogue what the future of open source organizations looks like and what might be possible because of them. Throughout, I'll offer you some hands-on tips for adopting these best practices in your own organization, no matter how open it currently is.

What follows isn't management theory. Rather, it is an empirical observation about how Red Hat and other companies on the cutting edge of management operate and lead. I'll share the lessons we continue to learn so that you, too, can thrive in an economy where all the old rules about how to lead the organizations of the future are changing. I'll also share stories about other companies and organizations, so you can also learn valuable lessons when thinking about building a passionate and engaged workforce. Over time, I hope these and other practices are ultimately codified into a new management paradigm. But I'll leave that to the academics. Perhaps these lessons can become a part of what business schools teach in the years to come.

I turn first to where it all starts—with igniting passion.

PART ONE

WHY

Motivating and Inspiring

2

Igniting Passion

When Red Hat first approached me about taking the job as president and CEO, the recruiter leading the search tried to describe the company's culture. He waxed on about the company's vision and its motivated workforce. Then he paused and said, "Do you remember the scene in *Blues Brothers* where John Belushi says, 'We're on a mission from God?' Red Hat kind of feels like that. These folks really believe they're on a mission to change the world." I nodded my head, figuring I knew what he meant. After all, I had been helping lead Delta Air Lines through its bankruptcy, which was one of the most difficult things I had ever done. I assumed that in that process, in which the entire workforce banded together to turn the airline around, I had experienced firsthand how having a purpose and passion can become a powerful force for change.

For generations, Delta has been an institution in the South—especially in the Atlanta area where it is now based. Everyone, including me, has always had a sense of pride working for the company. Even my mom was proud of me for working at Delta.

Generations of families have worked there. That's why, when the company faced financial problems in the wake of 9/11 and spiking oil prices, we all embraced a shared purpose that we weren't going to let the company fail on our generation's watch. We spent a lot of time driving home to everyone in the organization that we were in this together and that the sacrifices we were making through cuts to benefits and salaries were a necessary part of reaching our shared goal. The powerful purpose helped drive a deeper commitment to what we were working on as we fought through the bankruptcy.

But it wasn't until a rival airline swooped in with the intent to buy Delta after we had made all of those sacrifices to turn the company around that I saw something different in the eyes of my peers and coworkers. It was passion, pure and simple. Somehow the threat of being taken over by a rival lit a fire throughout the workforce. Employees, all on their own, began making and wearing T-shirts and buttons emblazoned with the slogan, "Keep Delta, My Delta." They were standing up and saying no. After all that we had been through, we weren't going to give up now. It was as if a match had been lit and the entire company rallied together to meet the shared threat of a takeover.

The remarkable thing was, it worked: in the face of the passion we all showed, the rival stopped pursuing the acquisition. The CEO of the other company credited Delta employees' massive outpouring of support as one of the main reasons he walked away from the deal. He said he was worried about the potential backlash to his own airline if he completed the deal. That moment concluded what was, for many of us, a deeply emotional experience and showed me the power of passion ignited in a workforce—a key lesson I brought with me when I joined Red Hat.

It Starts with a Purpose

Over the past few years, many authors have written about "intrinsic motivation"—things inside a person that motivate him or her, as opposed to external incentives like money or power. In their best-selling book, *Conscious Capitalism*, Whole Foods CEO John Mackey and Babson College professor Raj Sisodia write:

> *Business has a much broader positive impact on the world when it is based on a higher purpose that goes beyond only generating profits and creating shareholder value. Purpose is the reason a company exists. A compelling sense of higher purpose creates an extraordinary degree of engagement among all stakeholders and catalyzes creativity, innovation, and organizational commitment . . . Higher purpose and shared core values unify the enterprise and elevate it to higher degrees of motivation, performance, and ethical commitment at the same time.*[1]

Or, as the authors of the excellent book *Collective Genius* so aptly put it: "Purpose is often misunderstood. It's not what a group does but why it does what it does. It's not a goal but a reason—the reason it exists, the need it fulfills, and the assistance it bestows. It is the answer to the question every group should ask itself: if we disappeared today, how would the world be different tomorrow?"[2]

That's a message more and more companies are giving weight to. Having a purpose is not something just for tech companies or newfangled start-ups. For instance, the J.M. Smucker Company in Orrville, Ohio, which makes and markets everything from jams and jellies to coffee and peanut butter, has a stated purpose of "Bringing Families Together to Share Memorable Meals and Moments."[3] Or, consider the following diverse list of organizations and their stated purpose:

>*Disney*—"To use our imagination to bring happiness to millions."
>
>*Johnson & Johnson*—"To alleviate pain and suffering."
>
>*Southwest Airlines*—"To give people the freedom to fly."
>
>*Pivot Leadership*—"Better Leaders = Better World."
>
>*Charles Schwab*—"A relentless ally for the individual investor."
>
>*BMW*—"To enable people to experience the joy of driving."
>
>*Humane Society*—"Celebrating animals, confronting cruelty."
>
>*American Red Cross*—"Enabling Americans to perform extraordinary acts in the face of emergencies."[4]

Mackey and Sisodia also write:

>*People are most fulfilled and happiest when their work is aligned with their own inner passions. Personal passion, corporate purpose, and business performance all go together. For a passionate foodie, working for Wegmans or Trader Joe's or Whole Foods Market can be truly fulfilling. For outdoors enthusiasts, Patagonia, REI, and L.L.Bean are wonderful places to work. In such settings, work becomes so much more than a job. It even goes beyond having a satisfying career. It becomes a calling— something we were born to do.*[5]

For Mackey and Whole Foods, their purpose is nothing less than to change the kind of food and beverages each of us consumes so that we become healthier and live fuller lives as a result.

In Red Hat's case, its purpose and calling—*To be the catalyst in communities of customers, contributors, and partners creating better technology the open source way*—is built upon open source software (more on that later). But additional examples of how the dynamics of passion and purpose are changing the way work gets done come from other people and companies, as with Mackey and Whole Foods. Do you think a grocery chain could become as successful if the people who work and shop there didn't believe in the purpose of growing and eating healthy, ethically sourced food?

The same can be said of the open source community. Participants in open source decided they wanted a hand in the technology being created—that was their purpose for investing their time in creating better software. They didn't want to trust all of the work to the engineers sitting behind the walls of proprietary software companies.

For example, I send out personal e-mails to any Red Hatter who is celebrating a longtime anniversary—ten-year, fifteen-year, and so on—working with us. When I sent one to one of our top engineers, Mark McLoughlin, to celebrate his ten-year anniversary, he replied:

> *I think what's most gratifying is that after 10 years and the tremendous growth we've had, I'm still here for the same reason I joined in the first place—that Red Hat is a pure-play open source company.*
> *Thanks again!*
> *Mark.*

Making the code free and open was why top engineers like McLoughlin decided to work with us; they saw a job at Red Hat as a way to do good for the world. It's how Red Hat is able to attract the most talented people and engage them to the best of their abilities; we have a mission they believe in. Some companies dabble in offering some open source products, but Red Hat people are absolutely passionate about the fact that the only products we sell are 100 percent open source, which is something we all believe is fundamentally good for the world.

For context, software has long been a domain in which companies have tried to "control the code" and then charge customers to use that code. But Red Hatters are products of the "maker movement": people who embrace the decentralization of production. We see massive benefits to making the code free for everyone to use and benefit from. That helps explain why politicians and statesmen like the presidents of Brazil, Poland, and India attend Red Hat events. They see open source software like Linux as good public policy because they aren't forced to pay companies for the intellectual property associated with the code. That's why Linux programmers say, "Open source is not a matter of life or death; it's much more important than that."

But whether your business is to provide wholesome food or to write software that runs nuclear submarines, if you can create a compelling reason for people to participate, they will. The ultimate benefits of having a purpose, then, are that people work harder and turnover is lower than the industry average. As the authors of *Collective Genius* put it: "Purpose—not the leader, authority or power—is what creates and animates a community. It is what makes people willing to do the hard tasks of innovation together and work through the inevitable conflict and tension."[6]

More and more, executives and entrepreneurs are beginning to understand the importance of having a purpose in business—you need to have a goal in mind that transcends the profit motive. That's the only way you'll be able to attract the best and brightest talent. Think about the success that Tony Hsieh and his company, Zappos, have had, for example, by focusing on delivering happiness to their customers.

But what's less clear is that to truly perform at a peak level, simply defining a purpose is not enough. It's just a first step, the table stakes for competing in the twenty-first-century economy. What sets open organizations apart, and what gives them a true competitive advantage, is that they also have embraced the idea that they need to activate the emotional passions and desires among their workers to actually reach that ultimate destination as defined by their purpose. Today's workers want their work to mean something; they want to be part of something that makes a difference. If having a purpose gets people to do the right things, then passion motivates them to extraordinary performance—to go the extra mile—as they try to fulfill their goal.

Purpose is a baseline. But when you add passion, it's like pouring gasoline on the fire. That's what can take your organization to the next level of performance and achievement. As management expert Gary Hamel says, "To put it bluntly, the most important task for any manager today is to create a work environment that inspires exceptional contribution and that merits an outpouring of passion, imagination and initiative."[7]

At Red Hat, we realize that people invest their valuable time by choosing to work with us (versus the myriad other alternatives they have) because they want to feel as if they are changing the world for the better. Unlike my experience at Delta during the takeover attempt, Red Hat maintains an extremely high level of passion every day. It's not episodic or periodic: it's consistently there, bubbling, simmering, and sometimes exploding.

At Zappos, the idea of delivering happiness to its customers begins by focusing on first building a team that believes in the company's purpose. As Mig Pascual, a content developer for Zappos Insights, part of the Zappos Family of Companies, puts it, "Zappos hires talent whose personal values align with the company's core values, our employees have a genuine interest in helping others. They're inspired to be a part of something bigger than they are, and are able to fulfill their personal higher purpose at work by living out their own values every day."[8]

Red Hat associates passionately live our purpose every day, so it becomes the norm. I sometimes forget how different and special it is until someone new sees it. At a conference for Red Hat's European partners, the chief information officer (CIO) of a large industrial giant gave a keynote speech. During a dinner at the conference, the CIO leaned over to me and said, almost in amazement, "I have never seen a company of this size where the people are so passionate. Look at how much energy they have and how much they care, and this is just an internal event. You need to figure out how to bottle this!" That was not just gratifying to hear, but also eye opening because it helped frame for me how passion can be contagious and how it infects others around you so that they want to work and collaborate with you. That's why open organization leaders should look for ways to spur passion not just in response to threats, but also in repeatable and sustainable ways that create a competitive advantage for their organizations.

Rethinking the Role of Emotion in the Workplace

We often use the word "emotional" as if it's a bad word, especially in the workplace. You could argue that much of what we're taught about conventional management theory and practice is all about making the business world as dispassionate as possible. When people cry at their desks or explode in laughter in a meeting, they're often immediately written off as being "unprofessional." Why? Because emotions aren't clear-cut, they make things seem messy. Think back to the birth of social sciences like microeconomics, when economists used supply-and-demand curves to map out how people and markets operate. In science, we often make simplifying assumptions. In management science, the simplifying assumption is that people are rational, value-maximizing, unemotional cogs.

Think back to the Economics 101 class you might have taken in school. Your professor might have explained how certain simplifying assumptions are made to make the math work—assumptions that people are rational and that everyone has access to the same information. But toward the end of the semester, after you thought you understood what was going on, your professor confessed that the markets aren't really ever in equilibrium, there is no perfect information, and people are clearly not always rational. How else could bubbles and busts occur?

Conventional management theory makes similar (but inconsistent) simplifying assumptions because they are both social sciences that developed at a similar time in history. Management theorists had to make certain simplifying assumptions in which they stripped any kind of emotion or irrationality from the equation in order to make their models work. They needed people to act like cogs in a wheel, simply as inputs to a system that would create outputs. But, as we know, people don't easily fit such models, mostly because we don't act in the rational ways economists or management theorists think we should. A whole field of study, behavioral economics, has emerged to tackle this issue in the field of economics. We need the same in business.

Inspiration, enthusiasm, motivation, excitement—those are emotions, too. Aren't they generally considered to be positive things? Don't you want your workers to be inspired and engaged in what they're doing? The question becomes, then, do you really want employees to check their emotions at the door? The short answer is no. As a leader, you should be working very intentionally to spark as much emotion and passion as you can among your team rather than worrying about running the kinds of conventional management studies that try to measure how hard or fast people are working. While that form of management style may have worked well when workers tackled rote tasks like turning screwdrivers and working on assembly lines, it's completely irrelevant to modern workers. Today, we can use robots to complete mundane tasks. What sets the best companies apart from their competition is their ability to attract the kinds of innovative, intelligent, and, yes, emotional workers, who want to do far more than just show up and punch a clock. What open organization leaders need to do, then, is to challenge their people to take initiative, find ways to innovate, and gain an edge on the competition by getting them to all work together in pursuing a common goal.

Tapping into passion is especially important in building the kinds of participative communities that drive open organizations. The open source communities like Linux in which we at Red Hat work rarely emerge when there is no passion for the community's purpose. For Red Hat, that sense of purpose is driven by our passion to change the world by wholeheartedly embracing the principles of open source development.

The Leader's Role: Leading a Passionate Organization

The challenge for leaders is that—unlike financial planning, capital budgeting, or organization structure—there really is no formal management theory created to build, leverage, and measure passion among workers and other members of the participative community. Maybe the closest measurement is the level of engagement or even morale among workers, which companies typically gauge through employee surveys. While you can learn quite a lot from these measures—and we do use them at Red Hat—they can't easily capture exactly what I'm talking about. Unfortunately, it essentially falls into that ambiguous category of "You'll know it when you see it."

When I first got to Red Hat, it took me some time to adjust to and even make sense of the level of passion. I vividly recall, for example, conducting my first company meeting where I stood up in front of a group of Red Hat associates to answer their questions. But rather than pepper me with questions about the company's marketing strategy or the potential of the stock price, they asked things like, "What kind of operating system do you run your computers at home on?" "Have you ever used Linux or Fedora before?" "Do you have your RHCE?" (RHCE is a Red Hat Certified Engineer.) What these folks were trying to assess was not whether I had a handle on Red Hat's business model. They wanted to see how committed I was to the cause. Their hard-driving questions were designed to see if I was as passionate about it as they were, because they wanted to know if I would fit into the culture they had all built together.

After my first day of interviews at Red Hat, my wife knew something was different about me. She told me it was the first time my face actually lit up when I talked about my experience. I came to realize that I was excited about the potential of going to work for a disruptive company, one that was creating positive change in the world. That was something that, while I didn't know the nitty-gritty details about the technology yet, I could truly get passionate about.

A powerful awakening for me, I realized how motivating it is when a company truly has a positive mission and a purpose behind it. If you watch football on Sundays as I do, you'll notice commercials in which big-name companies talk about all the good they are doing in the world—regardless of what their business models might actually involve. As a result, the message falls flat; it feels false. As the old adage says, you can't put lipstick on a pig. That's especially true in our social media era, where it's just about impossible to fake authenticity. But when your organization really does have the kind of purpose that fuels a true sense of passion among your workers, it's electrifying—and that's something people even outside your company's walls can't help but notice.

As Bill George, former CEO of Medtronic, said: "Authenticity is not a characteristic; it is who you are. It means knowing who you are and what your purpose is. Your True North is what you believe at the deepest level, what truly defines you—your beliefs, your values, your passions, and the principles you live by."[9] That the company consistently makes the various "best companies to work at" lists is no surprise: it earns positive reviews from its employees for everything from its "small business atmosphere" to its exceptional work-life balance and delivers exceptional financial performance as well.[10]

Similar to Delta, our company has had moments when Red Hatters' passion exploded in the wake of threats from competitors and rivals. One great example predates me. Red Hat was blindsided by a longtime strategic partner that repositioned itself as a formidable competitor. At that competitor's annual industry event in San Francisco, where Red Hat had a booth and a sizable presence, the industry giant announced that it would begin offering a new Linux distribution, which was essentially the source code for Red Hat Enterprise Linux, stripped of trademarks and rebranded as its own "unbreakable" Linux product and sold at half the price.

That kind of news wasn't welcome on Wall Street, where Red Hat's stock took an immediate hit. Rumors even began to fly that its rival was about to acquire Red Hat as a way to take control of Linux as a whole. Overall, the situation looked grim. As Leigh Day, now vice president of corporate marketing and a longtime Red Hatter, remembers: "The whole company was just stunned, and there was a palpable sense of fear. Everyone was posting on memo-list [one of the internal e-mail lists], lots of speculation about what this meant for us as a company, and the question that kept coming up was, how was Red Hat going to respond?"

That's when a Red Hat engineer, Rik van Riel, jokingly posted that the company should trademark the term "Unfakeable Linux." In the conference rooms where the marketing and public relations folks were huddled, debating various responses, it was as if a light bulb went on. "It was so typically Red Hat," Day told me. "In came this great idea, the perfect response, from this passionate young engineer up in Westford, [Massachusetts], and we just ran with it."

Knowing that so many Red Hatters were on site at the event booth in San Francisco, a group from across different departments worked late into the night from the Raleigh headquarters to pull together a coordinated response. The next morning, visitors to our company's website saw "Unfakeable Linux" prominently featured on the home page. There were FAQs for the media and customers. At the competitor's event, Red Hatters proudly manned their booth, wearing red "Unfakeable Linux" T-shirts, ready to answer questions from customers and partners. Back in Raleigh, the design team had called T-shirt shops all over California until they found one open late that agreed to print and deliver the T-shirts to the events manager in a nearby parking lot that morning.

"It is one of my favorite Red Hat memories, because we had all felt so crushed by the announcement," Day told me. "We then pulled together, galvanized by this attack on our company and the open source way, and responded in an incredibly cheeky, coordinated, bold way that our competitor never could. Everyone, from our engineers to our designers to our sales people, were so proud to be Red Hatters at that moment."

What's remarkable is that this wasn't an isolated moment in Red Hat history. Every day, the passion of the people who work at Red Hat bubbles up to the surface. Take, for example, Jon Masters, a technology architect, who once gave a keynote speech at the industrywide Red Hat Summit while riding a bike that was powering the computer server he was using to give his presentation. "Working at Red Hat is one of the most rewarding and challenging jobs I have ever had or seen any of my friends have," Masters has said. "The unstructured environment is daunting at first, but over time it becomes exhilarating to have that kind of dynamic environment. The thing that really excites me is that there are always new challenges and opportunities." The passion is contagious. It's impossible to be around people like Masters and not be infected by the passion that pervades this place.

Make It Personal

Describing the value of a passionate organization is one thing; trying to build and maintain one is another set of lessons entirely. That's why a key part of my job is to help stoke that level of passion through my own actions. That means that when a new version of Fedora—a free community distribution of Linux—comes out, I try to be one of the first to download it and comment on its new features on our message boards. Sometimes my job means embracing the fun-loving and irreverent side of the business—like dressing up for our companywide Halloween party. A leader of a twenty-first-century organization is, in part, a "cheerleader-in-chief." Passion is an emotion, and it's tough to convey emotion in an e-mail or a company newsletter. Passion is, almost by its very nature, personal.

W. L. Gore & Associates, which has brought us breakthrough products like Gore-Tex, also credits breaking down the traditional corporate walls for helping the company continue to grow (it now has more than nine thousand associates in more than thirty countries and annual sales of more than $3 billion), more than fifty years after its founding. One of the company's associates once said, "The things we accomplish in business are very personal for a lot of us. It's not just that I've accomplished a business goal with a team, and then I can just go home and shut my brain off and go about life as usual. A lot of the other folks we work with become our friends and our family in a lot of ways, and when something good happens, we're going to celebrate the fact that we accomplished something. Sometimes, it's not just the destination; it's the journey."[11]

While all of this might seem somewhat silly to seasoned executives, it's all about breaking down barriers and showing everyone that we want them to let down their guard and let their passion rip. If purpose is about innate desire, then passion is adrenaline—the rocket fuel that propels people to walk through walls to make the place successful.

While I had tinkered with Linux before taking the job at Red Hat, I didn't have the deep appreciation for the power of open source that the people there already had, some of whom had laid the groundwork for the company's growth at the very beginning when it was essentially a bunch of developers working together. But what I could demonstrate was that I cared about what we could accomplish through open source, and that's something every Red Hatter takes to heart.

Most companies have a stated corporate purpose or mission statement. Unfortunately, these are rarely used words that do little to drive purpose or passion within the company. This is often because leaders do not feel that driving a connection to the corporate mission is part of their daily job. In open organizations, the connection is critical and can create substantially better performance in any company. A key job of *every* leader is to continuously create the context required for passion to emerge by connecting associates' job functions to the organization's broader mission. The good news is that it doesn't require a companywide mandate to get started. Any leader, in any company and in any function, has the opportunity to drive that connection. Connecting to the mission and showing personal passion can take any organization to a new level of performance.

Hire Passionate People

The level of passion in your organization is obviously correlated with how deeply your people connect with its purpose. As Simon Sinek, author of *Start with Why: How Great Leaders Inspire Everyone to Take Action*, stated in a TED Talk he gave in 2009, there has to be a reason, a purpose, for today's workers to commit and give their best effort for an organization. He continued:

> *Great companies don't hire skilled people and motivate them, they hire already motivated people and inspire them. People are either motivated or they are not. Unless you give motivated people something to believe in, something bigger than their job to work toward, they will motivate themselves to find a new job and you'll be stuck with whoever is left. If you hire people just because they can do a job, they'll work for your money. But if you hire people*

who believe what you believe, they'll work for you with blood and sweat and tears.[12]

For example, at Red Hat, we have at least three associates who are so passionate about the company's role in changing the world through open source technology that they have gotten tattoos of Shadowman, the elusive icon wearing the red fedora in our company logo. (Here's a bit of trivia: the red hat is an homage to our cofounder, Marc Ewing, who was known as "the guy in the red hat" during his time at Carnegie Mellon University, where he often wore his grandfather's red lacrosse cap. It's also a nod to several historical revolutionaries who wore red hats during uprisings.) How many companies can say the same? That's a level of permanence and sense of mission that no economist could ever have predicted with a chart. One owner of a tattoo, Thomas Cameron, a chief architect based in Austin, Texas, told me, "Regardless of what happens to Red Hat, whether it gets bought or even if I leave someday, it doesn't change my history. Yes, I have ink and it's because I am proud and humbled to be part of all this. I have come to realize how life-changing and beneficial to society this software we work on is. The mind-set and technology behind it is a way of life. There is a spiritual aspect to it. I hope and believe that the work and collaboration I have done has had an impact. I consider myself the luckiest guy because I get paid to make the world a better place."

Another powerful example is Adam Miller, who also has a Shadowman tattoo, which he got to mark his ten-year anniversary as part of the greater Red Hat open source community. Only Miller didn't work for Red Hat at the time! He actually worked for a big computer company with a household name. As you might imagine, his coworkers had a hard time understanding why he would do something as radical as getting a tattoo of another company's logo. "Red Hat, Linux, and open source in general really changed the course of my life in so many ways. It's something I've been passionate about for a long time," says Miller, who wisely got his wife's approval before he made his final decision.

While it would be wonderful if everyone in your organization and every new hire brought that same level of motivation and passion with them into work every day, that's not always possible. So how does an organization like Red Hat find people who believe in the same mission as it does?

First off, we have observed that the conventional interview process does a mediocre job of identifying if someone is truly a fit with our culture. While we can ask lots of questions to determine someone's skills and experience, it can be difficult to assess if they are truly passionate about the organization and our mission or just excited about the prospect of landing a job, any job. Culture fit is a hard thing to tease out in an interview. When it's core to your company, you must find ways to ensure that you're hiring the right people. When W. L. Gore makes its hiring decisions, for example, it looks for candidates who are driven, but not just by their desire to climb the corporate ladder. To help assess that kind of cultural fit, Gore relies on teams of its associates during its hiring process.[13]

Red Hat also finds passionate people by relying on Red Hatters themselves. The Red Hat Ambassadors program—an associate referral initiative—was started because we recognized that good people know other good people in terms of both their skills and their potential fit for an organization's culture. As the tagline for the program says, "No one can spot a potential Red Hatter better than a current Red Hatter." While Red Hat always had an informal referral program, it wasn't until we formalized the process by creating the Ambassadors program two years ago that we began to see internal referrals skyrocket from about 29 percent of all new hires to more than half.

Once again, the details of the plan did not come down from on high; a cross-functional advisory board assembled to lead the program's implementation. That helps explain why we went beyond the typical corporate approach of simply handing out cash rewards. What we have in place now is a structured program, similar to a tiered airline program in which you can achieve a different status based on how much you fly. In our case, we wanted to create an aspirational incentive plan that would reward associates for how many referrals they made that led to new hires. We asked associates what kind of rewards they wanted.

At the first level, a Red Hatter becomes a "Super Ambassador," earning a T-shirt and sticker for his or her first successful referral. It takes three successful referrals to reach the second level, where associates earn an extra 25 percent cash referral bonus, a sticker, and a coveted hoodie emblazoned with the words, "Mega Ambassador." Refer five people, and they attain "Ultimate Ambassador" status, which includes a onetime, 100 percent bonus match (effectively doubling the referral bonus), and the choice of either a cape or a jacket conveying that they are a Red Hat Ultimate Ambassador. In an annual drawing among Ultimate Ambassadors, they can earn prizes like a new bicycle; perhaps just as importantly, they are invited to join the program's advisory board. As a whole, the program has been a tremendous success in terms of both getting talent inside the company and feeding the collaborative energy we continue to stoke.

We haven't been able to completely eliminate interviewing people. But when I assess a candidate, I have changed the kinds of questions I ask. If you stick to only asking traditional questions during an interview—"Tell me about a situation where you failed?" or "Tell me about a situation where you were particularly collaborative?"—most people have scripted answers.

Instead, I focus more on asking about candidates' views on where their previous company is going and what they see as its future. How is the company positioned? I want to know if they have enough innate curiosity and analytical and conceptual skills to be able to frame strategically where they stand. A lot is about discovering if they are curious enough to care and want to know. I don't want somebody working for me who doesn't care. To me, curiosity also signals that the person isn't in it just for him- or herself.

By asking more macro-level questions, I can see where a candidate perceives the company as a whole moving, beyond just his or her individual role in that shift. If you're really trying to understand the whole business and clearly have opinions about it, that says you're not spending 100 percent of your time just making sure you nail your own job. It means you've clearly built relationships and talk to other people within the company. When someone brings that kind of perspective to an interview, that's a telltale sign that he or she has the potential to be a great team player.

Like connecting with a company's mission, this does not require a top-down corporate mandate. Almost all leaders have an opportunity to shape who is on their team—either by hiring or deciding who can transfer in or out. Recognizing that passion is a key criterion for a high-performing team and screening for that in your personnel decisions can bring tremendous value to your own team.

Recognize and Reinforce Passion

Another key aspect of building a passionate organization is finding ways to reinforce the kinds of behaviors you want to seed throughout the entire culture. One way that happens at Red Hat is through active internal message lists and e-mails, where the community goes out of its way to celebrate people doing great things.

An example of Red Hatters' passion comes from an e-mail by a principal software engineer, Stephen Gallagher, posted for the entire company in the midst of a busy—and stressful—time:

I just want to call out something I've seen today that makes me proud to be a Red Hatter. As most of the people reading this know, today has been a major crunch day in engineering. We're racing to land our final changes to prepare for the RHEL 7.0 beta and there have been many issues. Brew is overworked and taking hours to process builds; Bugzilla is slow, we're discovering new and fun bugs in errata tool . . .

And yet, as I watch this happening, I notice something interesting. While there's plenty of opportunity to be complaining about the situation, that's not really occurring. Development and Release Engineering are talking, helping each other out and looking for solutions to move forward. I see no accusations, no infighting and no snark.

This right here is exactly what Red Hat's culture of contribution and meritocracy is meant to inspire, and I just want to say "Thank You" to everyone that is living this ideal. You continue to make Red Hat one of the greatest companies to work for.

In turn, Paul Frields, the manager of Fedora Engineering, replied:

I couldn't agree more with this. When push comes to shove, Red Hat culture says we should go out of our way to help co-workers. That's precisely what I see going on, and I'm overjoyed by that. "When the times get tough, the tough get going" is a well-used cliché, but it's really appropriate today. Red Hatters rock!

Associates' willingness to share their passions so openly completely changes what it means to be their leader. I don't have to instruct everyone to "play nice" to make sure we meet our deadlines, because everyone already knows we are working together to accomplish something that is fundamentally good. During my first few months at Red Hat, I thought it was strange that I was being copied on many "thank you!" or "great job!" notes that the management team sent. This rarely happened at Delta or at BCG. But this behavior is embedded deep into Red Hat's DNA, where everyone tends to err on the side of over-thanking people and going out of his or her way to acknowledge the good work others are doing. When you have passion inside your organization as Red Hat does, a leader and manager's role becomes more about creating context and reinforcing what purpose and end goal the organization is working toward.

Having boundless passion for the mission is common in start-ups. You might even argue that it's a prerequisite to getting a business off the ground. But one of the challenges any organization has is how to keep the level of passion high even as it continues to grow and add new people in different locations. There are more than seven thousand Red Hatters, for example, spread among more than eighty offices and working remotely worldwide. To help stoke the flames of passion in every location, we have an internal employment branding team that celebrates the people and activities that drive company culture forward and then takes that culture external to attract like-minded candidates to our growing company.

A key project for the team is a quarterly video, "The Show," which captures the essence of some of the most interesting things, people, and happenings inside Red Hat worldwide. For example, "The Show" might highlight one Red Hatter who makes his own Iron Man Halloween costume using open source designs he pulled from the internet. Or, it might feature a profile of someone like Michael Tiemann, vice president of open source affairs, who, besides being one of the preeminent thinkers in the open source community, is also a music aficionado who built his own recording studio, Manifold Recording, using open source designs and software. We might also have a segment about the different ways groups of Red Hatters have given back to the community. "The Show" also highlights different Red Hat offices worldwide as a way to celebrate our international and cultural diversity.

Video is a much more powerful way to make these connections than just a corporate newsletter sent to everyone. It's a better medium for capturing the visceral nature of passion. And passion tends to rise when people are together. So, we work hard to make sure "The Show" is not just a link on the intranet that nobody clicks on. We promote it by holding a viewing party in every Red Hat office, where Red Hatters can meet people from other teams, connect with old friends, and laugh together at the video, while also enjoying food and perhaps an adult beverage or two. "The Show" even highlights some of the more creative parties that different Red Hat offices throw to watch the video.

In addition, we now set aside an entire week each year to celebrate our people, culture, and brand—"We Are Red Hat Week." While possibly sounding arrogant, it's really a purpose-driven exercise to reinforce what the company stands for and what we believe in—all of which got its start on Halloween in 1994 when Marc Ewing first released Red Hat Linux. We've continued that tradition by making Halloween more than just about costumes and candy; we now celebrate the culture of Red Hat. I dress up at the annual Halloween party during "We Are Red Hat Week" and perform a skit with other senior executives. It's like a team-building event or even like Homecoming Week at your alma mater; it's a chance to bond over shared experiences and to build anticipation for creating even more reasons to celebrate in the future.

The practice is fairly common at organizations that foster the passion of their workforces. Zappos, for example, holds a companywide meeting every quarter that is "like a high school play mixed with presentations about company updates. At this meeting, employees have an opportunity to showcase their talents on stage, whether playing an instrument, dancing, or singing. It may be perceived as all fun and games, but this production also has a huge team-building component that requires employees from all departments to collaborate and organize."[14]

By bringing associates together once a year to celebrate our identity as a company, we increase engagement, loyalty, and a healthy sense of pride, which will contribute to increased corporate revenue and growth for Red Hat as a whole. To accomplish that, we use an open source methodology and collaborative approach to build the content and the activities of the week, which range from games and volunteer events to the sharing of important company topics, such as corporate strategy, definitions of a brand, and product and technology insights. It's far more than just "spirit week" or a coffee mug for associates one day of the year. It's harnessing the essence of the company—our people, culture, and brand—and spending a whole week exploring it, connecting with each other, and becoming more in tune with who we are and what we stand for.

Each year, we focus on a theme based on where the company is. In 2013, for instance, the theme was unification among our more than eighty offices. In 2014, the focus was on moving forward together. Whatever the next twenty years throws at us, we can proceed with confidence, knowing that the best way to move forward is to move together.

Red Hat even leans on its community when deciding which charitable or nonprofit organizations to support. Donating money becomes another way to engage associates in the efforts they are most passionate about and meld their personal passions to what we do within the workplace. "We do it a little differently here, and the way the program came about and has grown is a pretty good illustration of our culture and values," said Melanie Chernoff, government and community affairs manager at Red Hat, who joined the company nearly eight years ago as an intern. Chernoff now chairs the corporate citizenship committee, which oversees Red Hat's worldwide charitable donations, associate matching-gift program, volunteer activities, and local community relations efforts.

Chernoff says that when she joined Red Hat after working for several years in the nonprofit sector, there was one committee in the headquarters office charged with charitable donations but no real strategy to determine which organizations would receive financial support. After she asked to join a meeting of that committee, her persistent questions and suggestions encouraged the other committee members to name her their new chair. "At Red Hat, if you have good background knowledge and have enthusiasm for something," says Chernoff about our meritocracy, "eventually someone will say, 'Congrats! This is now yours.' This is definitely a culture that allows you to follow your own personal passion."

In her new role, Chernoff headed up efforts to transform how Red Hat would give back, including sponsoring an anonymous survey issued to every associate about what kinds of organizations they supported personally and which they thought Red Hat should support. What Chernoff found was that Red Hat's associates made clear distinctions between the two. Where individuals might be passionate about the environment or art, for example, they felt the company should support organizations in four key areas: basic needs, health, education, and technology.

With those priorities identified, Chernoff again turned to the Red Hat community to best determine which organizations in those categories would receive the Red Hat's support. While there is admittedly executive involvement in the process in setting budgets, there is a strong commitment to let the associates run it from there.

"We are unusual in that we don't have a vice president of corporate citizenship or a foundation like many companies our size do," Chernoff says. "It is really about engaging our people, which is why we rely on associates around the world who volunteer their time to serve on committees." Red Hat establishes committees in the different geographic areas in which we operate. We give each a pot of money to distribute every year to best engage their associates in that area. The overarching corporate citizenship committee provides advice and support to the local committees as needed, as well as implementing matching-gift and volunteer programs that also rely on the power of the community, not just an executive team, to decide where to apply our efforts.

Once you give power to the community to make decisions, its members begin to apply that responsibility in interesting and powerful ways. For example, in 2008, when the economic recession hit and the holidays approached, it was impossible to turn on the TV or read a news story that didn't mention massive layoffs and the number of people who would soon be unemployed. While we were fortunate at Red Hat not to have to do anything that drastic, the notion of holding a large holiday party struck a sour note with many US associates whose family, friends, and neighbors were out of work.

That groundswell of support led to a change. Rather than throw a large gala event in Raleigh as we had done in the past, we instead held a modest party in our office. We donated the difference in what we would have spent on the party to a national charity chosen by associates. The US associates nominated thirty different organizations, and the North America committee vetted the nominations, selected five finalists, and put them up for a vote. That first year, the associates voted for America's Second Harvest, a national network of food banks; the program has continued in similar fashion with organizations like the Wounded Warrior Project, charity: water, Meals On Wheels, and Communities In Schools receiving our support during the holidays. The annual holiday donation is now one of the most popular company traditions with our associates.

Keep the Fires in Check

A leader's role can also involve keeping a passionate organization constructively focused when things begin to run amok, which they undoubtedly will. For some leaders, that could be considered a significant downside of introducing and stoking the emotions of the workforce. We have had disruptive battles flare up inside the organization when the "freedom fighters" face off against the "capitalists" over key decisions related to the kinds of technology we use at an enterprise level all the way down to the desktop. For Red Hat, these valuable debates impact our culture, but they are also times when our emotions can get the best of us. Sometimes, emotions make us lose sight of the facts in a situation—we tune out the merits of something we don't agree with. But, the upside outweighs any potential downside. We have worked hard to find ways to keep our emotions from overwhelming us. We have learned the value of hitting the pause button and having a difficult conversation about why we did what we did (something I'll cover in more detail in chapter 5). The point is that as an organization, we have had to learn how to best balance our passions so that they don't become destructive.

If you look through the right lens, every organization has the potential for world-changing impact. The role of a leader is to foster passion around that impact and to keep that passion alive by reinforcing it every day. In Red Hat's case that means advocating for the power of open source or championing its role in bringing positive change to the world. Our organization continues to pursue that purpose by making investments in open source beyond those required for our business, such as supporting free and open fonts anyone can use without the encumbrance of copyrights that would force payment for them. Red Hat's legal team tirelessly works to defend software freedom in the courts. We also support other organizations like the Software Freedom Law Center, the Electronic Frontier Foundation, and Creative Commons to show that we truly believe in the power of open source principles.

If your workers believe that what they are doing in their daily roles means far more than simply padding the company's bottom line, that they truly have an impact on the world in some way, what they can accomplish will be amazing.

Jim's Leadership Tips

1. ***Passion is contagious.*** Begin to personally display emotion, and others will follow.

2. ***Most companies have a stated purpose or mission.*** If yours doesn't, advocate to develop one. If it does, make sure you integrate it into your dialogue with others. It needs to be part of everyday discourse.

3. ***Add passionate words to your vocabulary at work, like "love," "hate," "excited," or "upset."*** It should be easy—you already use them at home. Others will start to use them if you do.

4. ***Add questions to tease out passion when you interview.*** Ask "what are you passionate about?" or "what inspires you?"

5. ***Create vehicles for people to show their unvarnished selves.*** Company outings or team-building events need to allow for some silliness.

3

Building Engagement

eaders at large, conventional organizations often ask me how it feels to lead an engaged, participative organization. That's a critical issue, especially because Gallup research shows that only 13 percent of employees worldwide are actively engaged at work, and more than twice that number are so disengaged they are likely to spread negativity to others.[1] Many executives see companies like Google, which gives away food and other perks, and think that building an engaged workforce is about lavishing things on your employees. Certainly perks like great sushi may get people to stick around the office longer, but they aren't in themselves tools that *engage*.

True engagement comes from, well, engaging. It's about leaders making themselves available for constant dialogue with employees. When I bring up this point in conversations with peers in the executive ranks, I often get blank stares and questions like, "That sounds like a massive time sink. It can't be worth it, right?" Or, "We've invested heavily in internal communications capabilities to discuss what's happening at the company." Or even, "Employees are welcome and encouraged to listen to our earnings call." I, too, used to struggle with how best to describe what we do at Red Hat as fundamentally different from simply proactively pushing out information to employees.

But I have come to appreciate that, as technology has automated rote tasks and as business strategies rely more on employees' initiative and innovative abilities, there is greater need for them to deeply understand and support the direction of the company. It's not just the changing nature of business strategies that are driving the need for engagement. It's the next generation of our workforce as well. Millennial workers have far greater expectations than their parents for being heard in the workplace. If you want to recruit the best and brightest talent and then keep them engaged in their jobs, you'll need to become far more accountable to them in terms of explaining why you made certain decisions, and own the results as well.

In their book, *Hidden Value: How Great Companies Achieve Extraordinary Results with Ordinary People,* Stanford professors Charles O'Reilly III and Jeffrey Pfeffer conclude that if companies create a culture in which employees take psychological ownership, even average employees can perform at high levels.[2] If employees feel that they are listened to and appreciated—that is, when they are engaged—great things can result.

Consider the Rochester, New York–based grocery chain, Wegmans Food Markets, which is renowned for its workplace culture, exceptional product range, and superlative customer service. As one employee noted during the company's application to a "best places to work" list, "I contribute something really meaningful. This company takes pride in empowering its people to a point where they do not feel like they are just 'doing a job,' they are actually playing a pivotal role in the company."[3]

I described the importance of purpose and passion in chapter 2; there is a tendency for managers to confuse these concepts with engagement. But purpose and passion are about creating meaning and excitement in one's work, while engagement is more about channeling that energy toward the specific areas that drive a company's success. It's about attention to the *whats* and *hows* of the company's strategies and tactics. It's about proactively being involved, curious, and questioning what the company is doing and each individual's role in making it successful. Put another way, if you want to build engagement, you need to stop thinking in a conventional organizational manner.

Purpose and passion go a long way to creating the motivation for being engaged, but neither creates engagement per se. There are obviously people who are very excited about the overarching mission or purpose of a company but fail to understand its strategy for achieving that purpose. Most people at Red Hat are passionate about open source, but that doesn't mean they are automatically engaged with the company and buy into the ways we are working to achieve our purpose. The leadership team and I must ensure that happens.

Many executives with whom I speak also confuse engagement with happiness or employee morale. Engagement isn't about being happy. Happy people may or may not be engaged in the business. According to Sue Moynihan, a director on the People team at Red Hat, companies tend to confuse "job satisfaction" levels among their associates with engagement. So rather than ask associates about how they feel about their compensation or benefits package—which are more closely tied to satisfaction—Moynihan's team measures associate engagement levels by tracking how many people react affirmatively to statements such as:

1. The people I work with are passionate about Red Hat's mission.

2. Associates at Red Hat take accountability for their work.

3. I believe Red Hat has a culture that allows me to learn and grow.

We also use a tool, Net Promoter Score (NPS), which has gained prominence throughout the business world as a way companies can ask customers if they would recommend their products or services to friends and family. At Red Hat, we've turned NPS into an internal tool and ask associates how willing they are to recommend working at Red Hat to their acquaintances, with the idea that only engaged associates would pass along an enthusiastic endorsement.[4]

None of the questions we ask attempt to measure morale or how happy people are. They measure knowledge of the business, how that applies to individual jobs, and perceptions of whether the rest of the organization is equally engaged. "If you're engaged, you're happier with your job, more interested in creating quality work, more productive, and more likely to recommend Red Hat as a great place to work," Moynihan told me.

At Delta, someone asked me, "What are you going to do about our morale?" My answer was, "Nothing." Morale is an output of many things. If employees believe in and are passionate about their purpose, have the tools they need to do their work well, and are engaged in what they are trying to accomplish, then they'll most likely have high morale. But the answer to low morale is to focus on purpose, tools, and engagement, not directly on trying to make people happy in and of itself. That's treating the symptoms, not the cause. People need to believe that the company and its leaders care about them. We see this theme in our survey results—Red Hat cares about its people, their workspace, their health, their needs. We are a community in that sense, and that's a big part of building morale.

If a key goal of the open organization is to build the capability for members to make their own decisions, act quickly, take initiative, and creatively solve problems, then engagement is critical. I've heard many times—and correctly, I believe—that a leader's primary job is to create context for his or her organization. As Howard Behar, former president of Starbucks, once said: "The person who sweeps the floor should choose the broom . . . We need to get rid of rules—real and imagined—and encourage independent thinking."[5] That is a powerful statement for an organization with more than twenty-three thousand locations worldwide, where thousands of its employees deal one-on-one with its customers. Having that kind of trust in an employee is a powerful statement that will, in most cases, bring out the best in that employee.

The department store Nordstrom is renowned for its exceptional customer service. When new hires join, they are given a one-page employee manual that states: "Welcome to Nordstrom. We're glad to have you with our Company. Our number one goal is to provide outstanding customer service. Set both your personal and professional goals high. We have great confidence in your ability to achieve them. Nordstrom Rules: Rule #1: Use good judgment in all situations. There will be no additional rules. Please feel free to ask your department manager, store manager, or division general manager any question at any time."[6]

That statement applies to leaders at every level of an open organization. It is dramatically easier and more effective when the people you are leading are proactively seeking that context. Similarly, initiatives aimed at offering greater transparency, information, and so on to all associates can be powerful, but if people aren't fundamentally engaged—if they don't care—then they really won't believe it anyway.

The Power of Engagement

My ah-ha moment about the importance of building engagement by communicating both the good news and the bad with your employees—and my conviction that this can be replicated at virtually any company—came when I was still working at Delta. Specifically, it was the day Delta filed for Chapter 11 bankruptcy protection. I was the chief operating officer at the time and responsible for developing and driving the turnaround plan. I had spent an exhausting several months either locked up with a small group of advisers working on the plan or in a New York conference room pitching our plan to raise financing from lenders.

The day the company filed for bankruptcy was horrible for every member of the Delta family. For me, it was also a crazy day of press interviews, calls, and meetings. At some point, I was asked if I would be willing to stop by the break room at the airport that night to meet with the night-shift line mechanics. Our turnaround plan included significant changes to maintenance in addition to pay and benefit cuts, so all of those employees would be negatively affected. I was running from one thing to another and, without much thought, I said, "Sure." I didn't realize at the time that the suggestion to go meet with those mechanics would become the best advice I've ever gotten.

By the time I arrived at the break room, I was exhausted. This wasn't a preplanned, prescribed event. As I walked in, I realized I had no idea what I was going to say, but there were a couple hundred people staring at me and waiting for me to speak. I decided that the best thing to do was to tell them the truth. I said that I was sorry and that the turnaround would require real sacrifices, but I also let them know that they were part of our holistic plan to revive the airline. I then launched into the same forty-five-minute speech about our plan that I had been giving to the bankers in New York for the prior few weeks. At the end, I apologized again, letting them know that management had failed them, but we had a plan to fix the problems. There was a lot of detail about arcane network and fleet concepts, but I thought it was important for everyone to understand how his or her sacrifices fit into the whole plan.

When I finished, I think everyone was a little stunned; at first, they just looked at me. Then they started asking questions—lots of them. Most impressively, the questions weren't about the pay cuts and benefits changes. Instead, people asked insightful and detailed questions about the plan itself. They were truly interested in how it would work and what they could do to make the plan successful.

I finally made it home and got some sleep, but word quickly spread about my trip to the break room. Suddenly, I had requests from areas across the company that wanted to hear the same speech. Those requests led to a more formal program that we called the "Velvet Rope Tour," where I joined other Delta leaders and spent time with groups of several hundred employees at a time, candidly sharing our plan and answering questions. Employees were pleased that the company respected them enough to share a high level of detail about our vision for Delta's future and how we came to the decisions we'd made. In turn, we saw a substantial jump in engagement, despite the fact that our employees' jobs were at risk.

Skipping ahead a few years, I was walking through the international terminal in Atlanta when two Delta mechanics approached me. They mentioned the speech I had given and thanked me again for laying out the plan, notably the details I shared about our intent to expand Delta's international presence. They had both taken that plan to heart and transferred to the international concourse, knowing they would be a big part of the company's turnaround. That was incredibly gratifying for me, and I had tears in my eyes as I thanked those two gentlemen and went on my way.

In the end, I garnered many great lessons from those experiences, such as:

- Bad or tough news is much better accepted when delivered in person. Be open and honest. Don't sugar-coat bad news.

- People thirst for context; they want to know the whats and whys of their company's direction, and they want to be part of making it successful.

- Being accessible, answering questions, admitting mistakes, and saying you're sorry builds your credibility and authority to lead.

All employees want a sense that their work is making a difference. They want to know how what they do is important to the whole. My Delta experience demonstrates that people are willing to make substantial personal sacrifices if they believe they are part of a broader plan for success. Leaders often underestimate the importance of creating that context and overestimate how much people know about the strategic direction of their organizations.

Engagement Is the Foundation

Of course, many companies and leaders understand the value of having an engaged workforce. What's different in an open organization is that it's not a "nice to have" overlay. It's actually a key component of the management system, especially as it applies to getting work done effectively. To put that another way, if you have an engaged workforce, it actually changes where and how you make decisions regarding what needs to get done. When you consider that thousands, if not millions, of decisions can be made within an organization every day, your ability to make faster and better decisions can have a massive impact on the competitiveness of your organization.

One major function of any management system is to effectively identify and react to changes in the marketplace. To me, the best articulation of this process comes from John Boyd, a US Air Force colonel and military strategist, who created the OODA loop. He originally conceived of OODA (observe, orient, decide, act) to describe the process a fighter pilot must go through to win a dogfight (see figure 3-1).

The idea is that we are constantly processing information that we observe—whether the location of enemy combatants or the actions of our competitors—before choosing to act on those observations. Therefore, the faster you can close the loop between new

FIGURE 3-1

The OODA loop

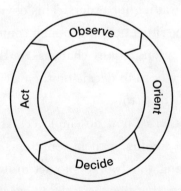

observations and take action, the more effective those actions will be. Consider the example of a fighter pilot flying a routine scouting mission. Out of the blue, he runs into enemy forces intent on shooting him down. That pilot might be required to report his situation to his commanding officers before he's allowed to fight back, which obviously puts his life in danger. If he's given more leeway to act on his own observations, he should be able to more effectively deal with the situation, based on those observations.

In conventional organizations, the OODA loop functions within a hierarchy that is similar to a pilot waiting for orders. Standardized management reports and communications working their way up the hierarchy through the chain of command are the "observe and orient" functions. Decisions are then made somewhere in that chain, and directions are subsequently passed back down for action. One risk of this system is that useful information is filtered or lost, and therefore important signals are missed. Another is the amount of time it can take for information to flow up, decisions to be made, and directives for action sent back. As the pace of business accelerates, those flaws are exacerbated.

But an open organization management system can be much more effective because, for the most part, it empowers the people making the observations to act on that information rather than pushing it up the ladder and waiting for orders. This obviously assumes that people observing the situation have enough context and knowledge to know what observations require changes. For the most part, pilots have the leeway they need to decide on their own actions, but they have been well trained for this.

An obvious question is, how do employees know when the barrage of information coming at them represents an opportunity or a threat? Empowering your workers to act unilaterally to changes they observe requires that they have the knowledge and context of the strategy so that they act appropriately. Engagement, therefore, is a critical element to the distributed management system we have at Red Hat.

Even so, isn't there a risk that workers will make poor decisions? Yes, but that's mitigated by the adoption of the open source principle of "release early; release often"—or "fail fast"—that entails tightening that feedback loop (I'll cover this in more detail in chapter 7). Here at Red Hat, people managers play a critical role in this process. They must determine the appropriate amount of latitude that each individual is capable of handling, plus develop, coach, and stretch their capabilities along the way. To make this work, everyone in the organization must have a sense of the strategy, why it will be successful, and how his or her individual actions can contribute toward those goals. But that's the definition of engagement, which is why having engaged employees is so important to the operation of an open organization.

Engagement also greatly improves another key management function—control. Not only are engaged organizations quicker to act, but they also require far fewer top-down controls. In many ways, the more engaged an organization is, the more self-policing it will be. If you no longer rely on conventional top-down management hierarchies to solve problems, you need to encourage and empower the members of your organization to solve their own issues. Consider how open source communities operate when there is no leader or group of leaders officially in charge. Rather, there are people who are charged with making decisions based on the input they receive from the group. When someone goes astray, the community itself resolves the issue. That's not to say that people can't be trusted. It's just that the more you are accountable to your peers, the more aware you'll be of the impact of your decisions and actions. That means employees and contributors are expected to work out issues among themselves, rather than bumping them up through the hierarchy for resolution, as in so many conventional corporate cultures. An open organization is focused on driving innovation and keeping ahead of market trends, not devoting scarce people power to missteps better left for peers to solve. Too many organizations tend to get sucked down into creating policies and procedures aimed at quelling misbehavior, which is truly a waste of a talented person's time and energy.

For example, if someone uses memo-list, our companywide e-mail list that reaches every Red Hatter, or any of our other internal communication tools in ways that contradict the values of the Red Hat community, he or she will pay a price. Managers at Red Hat coach their direct reports to work out their own issues, rather than immediately jumping in to act as mediator. "If you're a jerk and misbehave, you get frozen out and rendered ineffective and miserable, so there's a much higher penalty than a manager could ever induce for not being cooperative," said Máirín Duffy, a user-interface designer based in the Westford, Massachusetts office.

Similarly, Red Hat management trusts its community of associates to create ground rules when they're necessary. Sometimes, self-enforcement manifests itself in unexpected ways. An infamous story lovingly remembered as the "Bagel Touching Incident" involved an associate who took a bagel from a plate in the kitchen of the Raleigh office, then apparently decided to eat only half of it before returning the rest to the plate. When other associates noticed what had happened, they took to the Raleigh office e-mail list, which we call rdu-list, to decry the anonymous person's behavior. Someone also taped up a sign in the kitchen that said, "No bagel touching."

A similar incident occurred when one associate parked his or her car in a space reserved for a motorcycle. Within hours, pictures of the offending car found their way onto the rdu-list, along with associate-rendered ASCII-art diagrams and suggestions for painting better lines in the Raleigh parking garage.

Clearly, self-enforcement is not all about high-minded debate and grim punishment; it often involves humor and lightheartedness. But peer-to-peer management isn't just about enforcement; it's also a critical form of celebration and support. That means that every associate relies on his or her peers for the praise and acknowledgment that most companies give only their managers the power to bestow. "One of the things I appreciate the most about Red Hat is that we don't just call each other on our B.S.," Thomas Cameron, a chief architect, told me. "I am constantly impressed how often people point out when things go right. And it's not fake cheerleader stuff either. People will tell you, 'Thanks for kicking ass,' and really mean it."

Leveraging 360-Degree Accountability

In the conventional industrial model of labor management, managers managed and laborers worked. There was very little expectation that management would be accountable to labor. It would rarely have crossed a manager's mind to explain the rationale for decisions or directives. The mind-set was that workers would be equally efficient regardless of how much they understood about the company. In fact, they might be less efficient if they thought too much, slowing production lines and asking why. They were largely considered to be replaceable cogs rather than valuable intellectual assets.

Everybody knows what accountability is. In conventional organizations, accountabilities are clear, and they only go in one direction: up. Each person is accountable to his boss. That person is accountable to her boss. And so on. That's why accountability is neatly distributed and clearly rolls up. It's simple and scientific, and anyone who has ever had a boss knows what it is. But being accountable doesn't mean you have to ask for permission before you make every decision. It's not about saying, "May I?" all the time. Rather, it's about being accountable for a set of outputs after the fact.

So the simplest way I can describe the role of a leader in building, fostering, and enhancing an engaged workforce is to say, "You are accountable to everybody." That truly sets the appropriate bar for a leader's actions to driving deep engagement. For Chris Van Gorder of Scripps Health in San Diego, which employs more than thirteen thousand people in twenty-nine locations, managers are held accountable for quality, safety, and financial metrics, but also for people metrics: "I always teach at the new manager orientation that your biggest job in life is to take care of people. That is your job. If you take care of people, they will take care of you. But I also talk about responsibility and accountability. I am pretty harsh on accountability. My definition of accountability is, you can miss your targets once. You won't be here to miss them twice. Pretty simple."[7]

I and all of Red Hat's managers are accountable to everyone in the organization for:

- Knowing our strategy.

- Listening.

- Engaging.

To put that another way, my job is to explain not just what we're doing as an organization, but also why we're doing it. It's to inform and give context for our collective actions. My job is also to take questions and feedback and engage associates in a conversation about the decisions we're making as a team.

But the truth, it seems, is that most leaders and managers find it difficult to make themselves accountable at work for a couple of reasons. First off, it takes a lot of time to listen. You have to believe that it's part of your job description to invest your time that way. As soon as you think that's unproductive time, then it becomes brutally painful.

Early in my career, a senior partner in BCG's change management practice told me that, if you really want people to understand something, you have to tell them five times. I think she might have been conservative. Engaging with people takes a ton of time. You can't staff it out; you can't delegate it. You can use electronic tools to help facilitate communication, but you can't automate it either. It requires personal commitment. In the scope of the myriad other things that today's fragmented executives have on their plates, it's an easy one to let go. There's no immediate payback. The fruits of an engaged workforce come over time. You truly have to believe in the value, or you won't do it.

You won't hear employees if you've delegated the task of listening. I make the effort to personally answer every e-mail I receive from Red Hat associates, though I warn folks that it could take me a couple of days to respond. As a leader, your role isn't to tell people what to do but to tell people how they are important and how they fit in.

Unfortunately, few conventionally run organizations think about how they can use the tools they have in place, including e-mail, to create the kinds of two-way conversations needed to build accountability. At Delta, for example, I was the only executive who voluntarily gave out my e-mail address to every employee (and I did the same thing when I joined Red Hat). I made it clear that anyone could e-mail me anytime and that I would get back to him or her, if not immediately, in a reasonable amount of time. The result? It was as if I had unleashed the floodgates of pent-up demand.

I decided to share my e-mail address because, as I was walking through a maintenance hangar one day, one of the mechanics stopped me and complained that he had been using the company suggestion box, but clearly nobody was listening. Knowing that was probably the truth, I told the mechanic he could just e-mail me directly instead. But after doing this for one employee, I realized that I would probably get a lot of valuable feedback if I opened it up to everyone. It's next to impossible for a frontline employee to send a direct e-mail to top executives at any big, conventional organization. Which begs the question, why? In my opinion, feedback is a gift. I want and need to hear from folks throughout the company.

I once received an e-mail from a member of the airline maintenance department. The question required a somewhat delicate answer, so I tried to answer as best I could. I then received a response asking if I would be willing to discuss the issue further at a barbecue lunch the department was hosting the following week. As soon as I got that, I was intrigued. So I just picked up the phone and called up my new pen pal to tell him I would be excited to attend. After I explained who I was, there was a moment or two of silence on the other end of the line. "A few of my colleagues bet me that it wasn't really you answering your e-mail," he told me. That's exactly why it does matter that you, as a leader, open yourself up to everyone you work with.

While that's not always easy to do, there are systems you can put in place to help. Starbucks, for instance, has a program called "Mission Review," which encourages anyone in the organization to voice concerns about whether the company has strayed from its mission statement or guiding principles. The program has been a great success in that it generates thousands of comments from within the organization. Someone with knowledge of the issue or a member of the mission review team follows up on each comment.[8]

At Red Hat, I've needed to take my own level of responsiveness to a new level. Now, in addition to answering e-mails and occasionally responding to an important tweet, I hold informal town hall meetings in our offices worldwide to answer associates' questions. Yes, you can risk being overwhelmed at times, maybe even criticized or taken aback by questions about problems you thought had been solved. In my mind, that's how progress occurs.

Most leaders are wary of receiving lots of complaints. A number of Red Hat execs, especially when wanting to make a significant change, will groan because they know that they will have to confront the inevitable complaints, questions, and so on that come with working through changes. As one senior leader has said to me, "Everyone at Red Hat believes that it's their God-given right to complain about anything and everything." And frankly, they're right. It's part of what engagement is all about. It's painful and time consuming to hear a barrage of complaints, but the ultimate result makes it worthwhile. I'm fond of using the "it's like eating your broccoli" analogy. Going through the process isn't necessarily the most pleasurable experience, but it's actually good for you, and you'll feel better in the end. At Red Hat, we've all seen the results of the power of engagement. We all know it works and makes the effort worthwhile.

But it can be frustrating. Often, as a leader, you get excited to engage your people in the things you want them to focus on. You set up town halls, chat sessions, and so on, only to find out that your people want to discuss other things—things that you may not think are important or you simply don't want to spend time on. It's easy to feel as if those are a waste of time relative to the key issues you're trying to resolve. However, if these are the issues on people's minds, you need to address them proactively before they'll engage on the issues you want them to. It's a give-and-take, and ultimately you end up with better engagement.

The final barrier—and for many leaders, the most significant—is that it's never fun to admit your own mistakes. A painful experience for many of us, we'd rather avoid it. A study of a thousand leaders and employees conducted by Forum Corporation, a global consulting firm, found that only 19 percent of the employees it surveyed said their bosses were willing to apologize if they made a mistake.[9]

Why? The results showed that these conventional-style bosses were afraid of appearing incompetent or weak. Amazingly, 7 percent said they simply "didn't have to" apologize for making a mistake. I guess that makes sense if you fully buy into the conventional hierarchical organization as the only way to maintain order and get things done.

A good example of how I learned to be accountable to my team at Red Hat came in the wake of our acquisition of Qumranet. The decision was a bold step forward for the company into a white-hot sector called "virtualization," a technical term for describing how you can get a computer to run multiple operating systems at the same time. Buying the company gave us a leadership position in a key strategic area that underlies cloud computing. But while much of its technology was open source, key components had been written in another proprietary language and were anything but open. Our internal tech estimated that it would take about six months to a year to rewrite those pieces of code.

That left me in a dilemma. We had just spent more than $100 million to buy a company in a sector that was moving fast, and we would have to wait almost a year before deploying it. After weighing the pros and cons, I decided to go to market with what we had, with the idea that we would work in parallel to rewrite the code.

The end result was a giant dud. Not only did our associates hate using the product, they couldn't support it well because they weren't familiar with the code. Worse, our customers—who choose us because we are open source—didn't like it either. It quickly became obvious that I had made a mistake and that we would need to pull back the product and rewrite the code before we released it again. All in all, that mistake added up to about a year-and-a-half delay instead of a six-month one. But I owned it. I admitted to the company and board of directors that I was wrong and then hatched a plan to launch the product in a way that was true to Red Hat.

This example shows how essential it is to remain accountable to those affected by your decisions. Of course, there was quite a bit of anger and frustration among Red Hatters who wondered why the company was falling behind in the virtualization market. I realized that our associates deserved to hear the story of why we made the decision as much as the board did. When you don't explain your decision, people will often assume the worst: that you're detached, are dumb, or don't care. But when I explained the rationale—that my management team and I had, in fact, put a lot of thought into it—people finally understood. Red Hat associates appreciated that I owned my mistake; I earned their trust by explaining my decision— which also makes you a stronger leader. If you want to have engaged employees, in other words, you need to explain your decisions.

The key point for any leader is that you can build an enormous sense of trust and loyalty among employees when you actually take responsibility for your mistakes. For example, the Forum Corporation study also noted: "There can be no doubt that trust in leadership has a massive impact on workplace culture and business results. Employees that trust their leadership team are more loyal and efficient in their jobs. In fact, a solid foundation of trust can lead to increased productivity, profitability, and lower turnover."[10]

Being accountable to your employees is so much more than simply apologizing for your mistakes; it's about sharing the rationale for why you made any significant decision if the members of your organization weren't directly involved in making it (how to arrive at decisions is something I dig deeper into in chapter 6). As a leader, your responsibility is to create the context, framing, and explanation for why you chose a particular path. That means you'll be explaining yourself a lot, which can be really hard. Many CEOs complain about all the different "bosses" they have—from board members to analysts on Wall Street. You potentially have thousands of bosses in the guise of your associates and community members. Being accountable to all those folks is time consuming and emotionally draining. But when you do it, the payoff is enormous.

Generally, there has been an increase in the acceptance and importance of the notion of "corporate responsibility," where companies have become accountable to more than just their shareholders and the bottom line. For instance, companies have become more involved with the communities they work in—either literally, as in a town, city, or the environment, or virtually, as in the case of the Linux community. To do this, leaders have had to adjust their mindset about who and what they are accountable for.

To do this well, and at the scale we have at Red Hat, you'll need to work hard on how you communicate.

The Leader's Role: Scaling Up Engagement

Some CEOs believe in the power of proximity, where they want all their employees working in the corporate headquarters as a way to facilitate conversations (and likely to keep an eye on employees as well). At Red Hat, we think differently about how we connect thousands of associates, many of whom live all over the world. There are obstacles to connecting so many people virtually. More importantly, though, we have developed communications channels in a way that allows us to scale so we aren't hampered by the fact that our associates aren't with us physically. As Richard W. M. Jones, a principal software engineer at Red Hat, put it, "I don't think it makes that much difference, now that we're a company of more than seven thousand people, whether you're remote or in an office. The chances of me working physically near to people that I collaborate with is not high." In other words, just because a person sits next to someone doesn't solve the issue of how we can enable that same associate to communicate with an individual on the other side of the world.

In setting up employee communication systems, many companies make the mistake of thinking this problem can be solved simply by throwing technology at it. Executives who still think conventionally might tell human resources or IT to go out and buy collaboration tools. But, unless the company has the structure in place to let employees honestly talk to each other and their bosses, the tools won't help. So managers should first listen and then find the right communication tools. The grocery chain Wegmans, for example, has come up with a relatively low-tech solution it calls "Meeting in a Box," a template of talking points, videos, FAQs, and feedback-gathering tools that managers can use to facilitate conversations about everything from health benefits to the financial state of the company.

Low-tech "huddling" is also a common practice at any of the growing number of companies in the SRC Holdings family, an organization with more than twelve hundred employees and $400 million in sales, which originally spun out of a failed International Harvester plant in 1982. Much of what SRC does is connected to remanufacturing, or rebuilding everything from engine parts to electronics used in farm combines. It's the kind of work that requires you to get your hands dirty. But you can walk into any SRC factory on a given day and see hundreds of associates gathered around an easel or a whiteboard showing their daily or weekly huddles. The company's associates actively participate in understanding the health of the business by writing financial results on the whiteboards. That practice is part of SRC's famed open-book management system that uses transparency and financial literacy—along with low-tech tools like whiteboards—to deeply engage associates. "The meetings are, in fact, just one link in a chain of communication that is constantly moving information up and down the organization," writes Jack Stack, SRC's CEO, adding that when people are given information, they begin to see the big picture as it relates to meeting their targets, earning a bonus, increasing the value of the company's stock, and protecting their jobs. "One way or another, they are moving in the right direction and in the same direction," Stack said. "We are all working together to make those fractional improvements that determine whether or not we succeed as a business."[11]

Similarly, at Red Hat, despite being a cutting-edge technology company, we primarily rely on good old-fashioned, low-tech e-mail lists to help facilitate our conversations. We understand that participation is based on building that culture of accountability, not a set of tools. To help keep conversations on point, people can use separate channels. Over time, new associates naturally figure out what type of content belongs where. Here are a few examples of communication vehicles at Red Hat:

- *Announce-list*—An e-mail list for broadcasting information that probably won't need or require conversation. If a post generates more than one response, it will typically move onto memo-list.

- *Memo-list*—An e-mail list where we post informal things that will likely have a companywide impact and where we expect significant debate to occur. It's not atypical to have dozens or hundreds of messages on particularly important topics.

• *A topic-specific list, such as Cloud-Strategy-List*—Where associates most interested in cloud computing can discuss and debate topics in this area.

• *Blogs*—When someone has something really substantial and thoughtful to share, they blog about it. They know not everyone will read it, but it allows for much deeper exploration of narrower subjects.

• *Wikis*—When someone wants a more structured dialogue and more thoughtful feedback, the final weapon of choice is to use a wiki.

Conversations in these different channels can sometimes seem chaotic or even out of control. That's okay. As a leader, you need to learn to not police the chatter too much. If you do, you risk dampening its power. I learned this through experience. At one point, memo-list had become almost too polluted with nonbusiness-related items that many thought had simply gone too far. Some were sending out funny pictures of cats, and consequently people were starting to tune out the important items we wanted to share around the company. My initial instinct was to implement a set of rules to fix the problem. Fortunately, before my conventional organization top-down instincts kicked in, I got some advice from other veteran Red Hatters who suggested that I reach out to the most active memo-list users and posters and ask them to come up with the solution. And they did: they developed a set of guidelines and self-monitored the list, coaching people who were posting material that did not fit the role of the memo-list. They created another list for humorous material, because they recognized that associates, especially remote Red Hatters, wanted an outlet for sharing nonwork-related things with like-minded people. That was a key lesson for me in terms of learning how to foster participation without setting the rigid ground rules that tend to push associates away from contributing.

As a global company, Red Hat also had to turn to other solutions that help all of us stay connected as a whole and as parts of smaller working teams. Since even scheduling a room for an in-person meeting or arranging a global conference call can be complicated in an organization like ours, one of the internal teams put together a series of "connection tips" that highlight methods and approaches people use to connect and collaborate, combined with some perspective from the folks who actually put the tools to use:

1. *IRC (or instant messaging).* By far the most popular of all the tools, IRC is seen as a quick, casual, easy way to connect when you need to solve a problem or just stay in touch. "Instant Messaging (IM) is my lifeline. Sometimes just a quick answer is all that is needed and you don't want the e-mail to get buried. So having the ability for the fast connection is the best. I love that our team is all on IM and we use it constantly," commented Joan Richards, senior principal program marketing manager. According to Jennifer Scalf, technical account manager, "IRC lets me communicate with Red Hatters across the globe quickly. There are very few barriers; you can be anywhere chatting with someone else who is anywhere. Most of the time, whether it is in a channel or one-on-one with a person, the speed and effectiveness of using IRC to solve technical issues is amazing."

2. *E-mail.* Although some felt it wasn't always used effectively, e-mail has its place in collaboration efforts. "We use this as a fallback for when we can't get a hold of someone. It's really the slowest and least responsive of the technologies we use. But it's persisted across days/weeks/etc.," said Jason Connor, senior software engineer. Stephen J. Smoogen, Fedora team, added, "Always default to e-mail. It is a recorded media, it can be kept as a local copy, and it can hold a lot of data which might not be easily communicated in IRC or other things."

3. *Elluminate.* The web-conferencing program is a great tool for sharing presentations and keeping a recorded copy. "I love to use phone and Elluminate (and recording for replays). I'll share desktop/browser and slide deck to discuss topic of training session and allow real-time Q&A and demo of new feature/function in product releases," commented Cliff Perry, manager of software engineering.

4. *Etherpad/social intranet.* These tools, which include one called Mojo, provide a lot of interaction and online collaboration on documents and notes. According to Peter Larsen, solution architect, "I use Mojo [our social intranet platform] to allow collaboration in regards to official documentation, presentations, etc., that I share with my peers (or they with me). We'll communicate on e-mail/IM/IRC and share links to information on Mojo that we then work on."

5. *Video conferencing.* Although sometimes the hardest to use, video conferencing helps generate a feeling of being there when face-to-face isn't possible. "We have once-a-week meetings on video chat. It helps to see people's faces and facial expressions . . . even though the same information could

be communicated on IRC or e-mail. It takes a bit longer, but it is worth it," said Michael Foley, quality engineering supervisor.

The good news about using simple technologies is that you don't have to wait for a corporate mandate or major program to implement a collaboration suite. Any group, department, or function can leverage existing tools to engage. Creating a departmental mailing list is generally easy to do. It's not the technology that drives engagement. It's the commitment of the leader to truly engage.

Scaling Engagement

Red Hat also works to scale engagement beyond its walls and beyond the software sector itself. To that end, we launched a site, opensource .com, in 2010 (we had owned the URL for many years) because we knew there were many inspiring stories about how the principles of open source—collaboration, transparency, meritocracy, and so on— were being leveraged beyond the software industry. Our hope was to create a place where anyone could learn about and share stories of the growing open source movement.

We call opensource.com a "Red Hat community service" because we provide the hosting and editing for the site. But the content— articles about how the open source way has woven into areas such as government, education, health, law, and life—comes from our extended community, which includes Red Hatters. Over the years, the most popular articles have covered a range of technical topics, such as a discussion about the top open source project management tools. But the site has also tackled everything from how open source helps libraries to how it might provide a solution to the problem of bee colony collapse.

Since launching the site, we have shared thousands of diverse open source stories and have gathered an impressive following. We've published thousands of articles and generated millions of page views. On social media, we have tens of thousands of Twitter followers and Facebook fans. We're also growing our Google+ community and LinkedIn professionals group.

Jason Hibbets, who spearheads the effort for Red Hat, has worked to build a diverse and growing community that already numbers hundreds of authors, some Red Hatters but many who are not. Additionally, the most engaged community members have taken on the role of community moderators and are leading the continued evolution of the site. These volunteer moderators don't work for Red Hat, but have a personal interest in the open source way. They contribute their time to write articles, engage with commenters, and spread the word about content on social media. "Opensource.com is a great example of the open principles of catalyzing a community and building a platform that engages other people," says Jeff Mackanic, Red Hat's senior director of global awareness, who was instrumental in launching the site.

While this community has helped plant the seeds of open source awareness, there is much left to do. The door is open for the open source way to bring success to nontechnology companies, schools, universities, governments—to the world. I eagerly await the day when the open source way becomes the expectation rather than the exception. Opensource.com is a place where we can shine a light on the progress along the way, thanks to our active participative community.

Go All the Way . . . or Don't Start

When collecting feedback from employees and customers, many companies still rely on an age-old standard: the suggestion box.

Usually it's some kind of locked box stationed somewhere in the break room or similar area where management encourages people to tell it how the business could do better. The idea, of course, is that management collects the ideas and complaints regularly and then addresses the most pressing issues or even the best ideas.

But we know what really happens with the suggestion box. Nothing. I recall watching a television program on one of the food channels that features restaurant turnarounds. I'm sure you know the format: a famous restaurateur parachutes in to save a struggling business. In this particular episode, the struggling business owner pointed to a suggestion box as proof that he was listening to his employees and customers. Not only had the restaurant owner not bothered to check the contents of the box in some time, he had actually lost the key to it. The consultant used a sledgehammer to open the box as the camera zoomed in and dozens of ignored suggestions floated to the floor.

The worst possible thing is if employees contribute their best ideas and nothing happens. Listening is simply not enough. Or the HR department runs the effort without any other senior leadership involvement. That tells your people not to bother. Soliciting feedback and ignoring it is worse than not soliciting it at all. But it takes time to do things the right way—a lot of time.

Accountability plays a huge role in building a collaborative and innovative workplace. While you might go through the motions of putting out a suggestion box so your employees and customers can speak up and connect with you, it won't mean a thing unless you're serious about it. Ignoring your suggestion box will only push your employees further away, creating the kind of cynicism that becomes difficult to reverse. Employees simply won't trust that you're really listening.

While much of the feedback might not have any intrinsic value in isolation, the overall benefits are huge. Not only do you get a few good ideas, but, more importantly, you also get deep engagement from your employees. They will feel as if they are part of a living, breathing system, not mere cogs in the wheel.

Jim's Leadership Tips

1. *Enter every interaction with people in your organization believing that each person is equally accountable for his or her contributions and performance to everyone else, regardless of reporting relationship.*

2. *If your boss is not providing the appropriate context, ask for it.* Most bosses are happy to share. They just haven't yet figured out that it's part of what they should be doing.

3. *Understand the tools and vehicles your company has for internal communications.* Use them or advocate to get better ones.

FOR PEOPLE MANAGERS

1. *Use every interaction as an opportunity to share context and knowledge.*

2. *Equip your team with the skills and knowledge to be successful.*

FOR INDIVIDUAL CONTRIBUTORS

1. *Don't wait for your manager to provide context.* Be proactive. Understand your company's strategy, and do what you can do to make it successful.

2. *Engage with your peers.* Learn from them and let them learn from you.

PART TWO

HOW

Getting Things Done

4

Choosing Meritocracy, Not Democracy

Most people understand how decisions are made in a hierarchy. You don't have to know the specific people in the organization. All you have to see is the organization chart. In general, the higher on the chart, the more say a person has. If an issue cannot be resolved at one level of the hierarchy, it moves up until there's just one decision maker. It's neat and orderly. But what happens when you work in an organization that isn't a top-down hierarchy? Who makes what decisions? How are disagreements adjudicated?

Red Hat still has organization charts, but how we make decisions doesn't necessarily follow that structure. We have modeled ourselves less on the familiar, traditional corporate hierarchy model and more on what the ancient Athenians, the founders of democracy, called *politeia*, a term they used to describe their society. To be a member of the Athenian *politeia*, according to the authors of *A Company of Citizens*, meant that you thought, argued, and acted with your fellow citizens, and that you learned through the practice of civic life. Each person was actively engaged in learning and seeking a common purpose. In other words, the Athenians lived in what they called "a community of citizens," which was built upon a meritocracy.[1] That system, when applied within a company of citizens, would be based on this recognition:

> *Merit means that decisions are based on the best case put forward; excellence, not position, prejudice, or privilege, is the criterion for choice. In a company of citizens, the best case for action is that which carries the day after the open, sufficient, and informed debate. Merit means that every thoughtful and knowledgeable individual, with good ideas based on real understanding, will get a hearing. The incompetent blowhard will not. The practice of merit gives lie to the idea that participatory democracy must devolve to the lowest common denominator.*[2]

Similarly, the primary responsibility for leaders at Red Hat is to build and support our meritocracy by making sure the right people are working together on the right things. The people who are closest to the issue, rather than those responsible for the overall direction of the organization or team, tend to make the decisions. This requires collaboration and mutual respect between associates and their managers, in a complementary relationship. We try to have the right people in charge of the right decisions and hope they have the humility and organizational understanding to be open to influence and outside perspectives.

For example, at Stew Leonard's, a chain of food stores in New York and Connecticut that is famed for its exceptional customer service, literally every employee can do whatever he or she needs to—from answering questions to rejecting faulty merchandise—to ensure customer satisfaction without having to first get approval from management.[3] Similarly, at Red Hat, we strive to ensure that the people most capable of making the decisions, regardless of their title, make the vast majority of our decisions. But that raises two questions: Who is empowered to make a decision? Who decides who is empowered to make a decision?

It's Not a Democracy

Many people assume that if an organization is not top-down, then it must be some flavor of democracy—a place where everyone gets a vote. In both hierarchies and democracies, decision making is clear and precise. It's proscribed and can be easily codified. In most participative organizations, however, leaders and decision making don't necessarily follow such clear rules, just as it was in ancient Athens, where literally every citizen had the same opportunities to lead or follow others. Some people have more influence than others. Some people state an opinion and quickly get others to fall in line. It's not because they have positional authority. There is something else at work in these organizations. We've all seen it elsewhere, whether it's a teenage daughter coping with the "queen bee" phenomenon or a social group in which there are one or two people who clearly run the show.

Exactly how leaders emerge and get others to follow in voluntary organizations has been the subject of much research and writing, which is far beyond the scope of this book (though I do recommend reading *A Company of Citizens* for more details on ancient Greek society). But it's important to recognize that informal leaders do emerge. And in less structured, less hierarchical organizations, they are a key part of the overall management system.

At Red Hat, some of the seven thousand voices inside the company have far more sway than others. In most cases, decisions aren't made by executive fiat, nor are they arrived at through consensus. Rather, those people who have earned their peers' respect over time drive decisions. Associates who make a positive impact on the business and on the culture find that they gain more influence than those who do not. That's why we call our culture a "meritocracy," which, if you use Wikipedia's definition, means:

> *A system of government or other administration (such as business administration) wherein appointments and responsibilities are objectively assigned to individuals based upon their "merits," namely intelligence, credentials, and education.*[4]

Michael Young coined the term in 1958 in his book, *The Rise of the Meritocracy*. Strangely enough, Young used the term satirically as he described a dystopian future where a person's place in society would be linked to his or her scores on standardized tests. But the term has evolved to take on a deeper, more positive meaning. For example, when Liz Elting, cofounder of TransPerfect (the parent company of Translations.com), was asked how her business has grown into a $350 million company with two thousand employees, she credited the culture of meritocracy they have created:

> *We did not know from day one how this meritocracy would develop or what the best practices would be. What we did know was that a meritocracy was the only model we felt we could truly believe in and fully support. We created a foundation of accountability that not only gave our employees the motivation to succeed, but also*

presented management with clear opportunities to unequivocally note an employee's success. By holding each individual responsible for their goals and role within the company, we have been able to empower each member of TransPerfect to take ownership of their contributions and truly demonstrate their value. This core idea helped drive our very first employees; 2,000 people later, it continues to drive our business today.[5]

Within the meritocracy we have built at Red Hat, everyone has the right to speak and access the kinds of tools that will help ensure that his or her voice is heard. But to appreciate how a meritocracy works, you need to first recognize that not everyone is listened to *equally*. That is to say, everyone has an equal chance to be heard, but the meritocracy functions so that the collective helps empower and choose the leaders and influencers.

At most companies, everyone knows who the "A-players" or "superstars" are, even if their title doesn't necessarily convey how much influence they have within the company. When I worked at BCG, we used the terms "thermometers" and "thermostats" to categorize people in an organization. *Thermometers* are people who reflect the temperature (hot, cold, or lukewarm) of the organization; the *thermostats* are the ones who set it. When it came time to create change in an organization, we knew we needed to get the thermostats on board to help drive those changes by setting a new temperature that would be quickly reflected by the thermometers.

The challenge for most companies, though, is that while everyone knows who the thermostats are, it's very rare that anyone takes real advantage of his or her potential influence. The challenge and the opportunity for companies and organizations, therefore, are to find ways to not just openly recognize the thought leaders, but also to leverage the thermostats to drive innovation and decision making forward. When it's time to make big decisions or get people on board with new initiatives, you need to find ways to get the thermostats involved in the action as early as possible. That's how you can help ensure your best chances at success.

An example of how we leverage our thermostats at Red Hat is Máirín Duffy, a user-interface designer. Duffy started working at Red Hat as an intern and later joined full-time in 2004 after she graduated from college. While Duffy has made exceptional contributions to the core Red Hat Enterprise Linux product, she has also earned a stellar reputation throughout the company for her reasoned and intelligent contributions to memo-list conversations on everything from the creation of the mission statement to the adoption of certain controversial proprietary software programs. In a case involving the latter, DeLisa Alexander, executive vice president and chief people officer at Red Hat, approached Duffy to talk about such a proposed project. "DeLisa approached me in person—I had never met her in person before—because she knew from memo-list how vocally I was against Red Hat using proprietary software," Duffy said. "She had caught wind of such a project and let me know about it, asked me what I thought, and supported my efforts to have it reconsidered. It eventually was and didn't move forward then as planned. The people who take the initiative to make sure the right thing happens are the ones who end up winning the influence."

This is an example in which a senior leader in the company went directly to someone working close to the frontlines to gather feedback on a fairly major corporatewide decision simply because Alexander, the executive, knew that Duffy, the designer, could help make or break the success of the final decision, based on her level of influence throughout the company. That's how a meritocracy functions.

The Open Source Way:
Leadership Is Earned

The first questions in building a meritocratic system are: How do you decide whose ideas get more time and attention? How do you assign merit in a modern corporation? Why would the opinion of someone like Máirín Duffy merit the attention of a high-level executive? Or, how does a fifty-year-old company like W. L. Gore continue to be successful despite the fact that it has a uniquely egalitarian culture in which there are very few traditional job titles and even fewer people considered to be bosses in any traditional sense?"[6] The answer is surprisingly simple. To become a leader in a meritocracy, you need to attract followers first, not the other way around, as is typical in most conventional organization structures. Your peers actually have to select you as their leader based on how effective they think you are, not just because you have a more impressive title or résumé.

For newcomers to Gore's culture, especially those accustomed to a more conventional corporate environment, joining the company can be a somewhat daunting experience:

> *"When I arrived at Gore, I didn't know who did what. I wondered how anything got done here. It was driving me crazy." She also didn't know how to work without someone telling her what to do, and kept asking "Who's my boss?" "Stop using the B-word," she was told. She also saw that people didn't fit into pre-defined job slots; they had team commitments that often combined roles traditionally done by different departments. It took a long time to get to know people and what they did, and to earn the credibility and trust required to be given responsibilities. But she did, and eventually went on to become what she calls a "category*

champion." Her experience is the norm. Another associate with 20
years of experience on multiple teams, observed: "You join a team
and you're an idiot . . . It takes 18 months to build credibility. Early
on, it's really frustrating. In hindsight, it makes sense."[7]

Red Hat's culture and management system, which relies heavily on open source principles, is similar. A common saying in open
source is, "The code talks." In other words, the folks who earn the
most influence in any open source engineering project tend to be
those individuals who contribute the best code or new ideas, or even
have a gift for spotting bugs. There really is an objective beauty to
this principle because titles, experience, and politics begin to matter
far less than insight and sound reasoning. That's how the best ideas
get acted on rather than the most popular ones, which is a subtle but
extremely important difference.

Red Hat has built upon this concept as well. Sure, our engineers
earn influence with each other based on their contributions to the
code. But the same principle applies to all associates in the organization, regardless of what department they work in or what their
day-to-day job entails. Everyone has the ability to earn influence and
to get his or her ideas heard. It simply relates to how effective you
are at presenting and getting people behind your ideas, throughout
the organization.

Red Hatters like Máirín Duffy build their reputations and influence through sustained contribution. That means doing a great job,
but also helping others and contributing to the multitude of internal
discussion threads that are ongoing at any one time. Some associates post a lot of their opinions, while others are more judicious in
the number of discussions they weigh in on. But the path to building influence really is about quality over quantity. Frequent posters
may find that they lose influence if their peers begin to treat their

contributions as mere noise. It's like living in a small town where, no matter how much you try to hide, everyone knows quite a bit about you based on how you live your life.

Successful open source software projects—and, by extension, open organizations—are those in which the most influence over the direction of the project lies with the people who contribute the most meaningful work. In other words, projects and organizations work best in the context of a meritocracy. How, then, does this principle manifest itself at Red Hat? Who decides who leads and who follows? To answer these questions, we've taken a page from the open source manual and allowed a meritocracy to grow.

Building a Culture of Thought Leaders

While most company hierarchies dictate who gets heard, the most influential voices at Red Hat aren't necessarily tied to someone's title or even his or her longevity within the company. Instead, the most respected individuals tend to be those who have a track record of being consistent and selfless. You can't assume that your job title gives you credibility, any more than it does in a real community. People might watch you a little more closely because of it, but they're looking for their own clues and assessing your importance by their own criteria.

At Red Hat, you also can't gain influence or followers by gaming the system, as we often see in conventionally run organizations. We're all familiar with the folks who get labeled brownnoses or similar as they climb the ranks of political and bureaucratic hierarchies. They are the political animals in the organization. They make friends and allies mostly to help advance their own careers. Yet, while everyone knows who they are, they still seem to get their way, because conventional bosses respond to that kind of sycophantic behavior.

It's much harder to manipulate an open organization community like Red Hat's. There are too many people who will flag you for being insincere, and your reputation will suffer. Those people who are the most committed to the mission and purpose of the organization, on the other hand, and who work hard to fulfill its goals are those whose voices become the most predominant. So when I run into Thomas Cameron from time to time, I listen to him because I respect the brand and reputation he has built within the company, not because he's trying to butter me up. At Red Hat, we revere our influencers wherever they work. That's the essence of a meritocracy.

A meritocracy also means that you don't need people reporting to you to create change and get yourself heard—a notion that many organizations struggle with. Rebecca Fernandez, a senior employment branding specialist at Red Hat, explained it in her article "Building a positive meritocracy: It's harder than it sounds":

> Most people have experienced the Peter Principle in action: In a hierarchy every employee tends to rise to his level of incompetence. In other words, people are promoted so long as they excel. When they are promoted to a position where they lack competence, they stay there, unable to gain further promotion and unlikely to be demoted. This happens because upward mobility generally involves a move into management. The brilliant engineer becomes the bumbling manager . . . To create a positive meritocracy, we must re-envision management as a career track parallel to others (e.g., engineering or marketing), with overlap for some dual-skilled candidates.[8]

At Red Hat, we address the dangers of the Peter Principle by offering ways for an individual to grow his or her scope and influence without having to change jobs. The people who are listened to have earned the respect of their peers, regardless of their position or role in the company. Because of that, associates can grow their role tremendously without being promoted up the hierarchy, by simply continuing to build their own credibility and leadership brand. Jan Wildeboer, a Red Hat veteran whose official title includes the word "evangelist," is an example of a nondeveloper who is a key influencer. Wildeboer, who is fond of wearing a red fedora (given to every new hire) just about everywhere he goes, has substantial influence not just within Red Hat, but also within the greater software community. His passion and energy for open source earned him his title, which is a great gig if you can get it.

Red Hat works to enable careers of *achievement* as well as careers of *advancement*. In conventional organizations, though, it's all about advancement—how far you can climb the corporate ladder in order to gain the kind of power and influence you crave. But what often happens is that some of the best people may not want to advance in that way. If you are a top software developer, for example, the only way you can get promotions, raises, and increase your influence in a conventional organization is to get promoted into a management role, even if you happen to hate the idea of managing other people and regardless of whether you are even good at it.

That notion is turned on its head in open organizations like Red Hat by promoting the idea that people can excel and achieve what they are best at and still build influence, without necessarily having to do a job that they may not like as much or be as good at doing. The people with the most influence in our organization are not necessarily those who hold fancy titles or have people working for them.

For example, Wildeboer's role—along with others like him, such as Michael Tiemann, vice president of open source affairs—is really to serve as an educator about what open source software is, Fedora and Red Hat Enterprise Linux specifically, and how it can help transform everything we know about software. These aren't necessarily the roles these folks were hired for; more often, this kind of job is earned. The core open source programmers and developers worldwide would never accept some charlatan or slick salesperson advocating for their cause. Wildeboer and Tiemann earned their reputations and influence and, hence, have pivotal roles in steering the future of open source. In this way, they also add immense value to Red Hat, helping build the company's reputation in the open source community.

In the conventional organization, recognition and rewards are just another top-down process that managers initiate. But at Red Hat, we have long appreciated the power of peer recognition to fuel meritocracy. For many years, the Red Hat Reward Zone program has enabled associates to recognize and reward peers who go beyond what's expected. Each quarter, regardless of rank or seniority, every Red Hatter—myself included—is granted an equal number of points to use for rewarding fellow associates, who can redeem the points for gift cards and other merchandise. Sometimes we use Reward Zone awards to recognize peers for extraordinary efforts, such as working late at night to help someone else find a solution for a customer. Associates also reward peers for living our values and doing things the Red Hat way, such as inviting other teams to contribute their ideas and feedback on a project. One of the most popular reasons for giving and receiving a Red Hat Reward is collaboration—a powerful reminder of how essential that ingredient is to company culture.

Another example of how we work hard to recognize those Red Hatters who best exemplify company values and culture is the Chairman's Award. Started several years ago by former chairman and CEO Matthew Szulik as a way to drive a culture of peer recognition, the Chairman's Award is the highest honor you can earn at Red Hat. It's also very difficult to win, since you need to be nominated by at least two of your peers (not your manager). Only about seventeen people earn the honor each year. When someone wins, we celebrate by treating him or her like an all-star at our annual Red Hat Summit and by creating a video in which that person's peers talk about all the reasons he or she deserves the award. When you add all that up, it's easy to recognize why it's a powerful force that works from the bottom up and reinforces everything the open organization is built on—connection, trust, transparency, collaboration, and meritocracy.

The Leader's Role: Empower Your Rock Stars to Follow Their Passions

Freeing up the thought leaders and rock stars can jumpstart innovation, something every company and business is trying to bottle. Companies try many things to drive innovation. One example is Google's approach. Ever since Google became more of a household name starting around 2004, business leaders and thinkers have been digging to find out the company's secret sauce in an effort to replicate its spectacular success. One of its best-known, though now defunct, programs was one in which all Google employees were encouraged to spend 20 percent of their time on just about anything they wanted to. The idea, of course, is that by empowering employees to pursue projects and ideas they are passionate about beyond the day-to-day duties of their real job, breakthrough innovation will follow. The company can even tout how, before it ended the program, successful side projects like Google Suggest, AdSense for Content, and Orkut all emerged from these 20 percent efforts—an impressive list, to be sure.[9] I applaud Google for taking such a far-reaching approach. Given Google's phenomenal track record of innovation, it's no surprise that companies of all shapes and sizes have tried to duplicate this model in attempts to drive innovation throughout their organizations.

At Red Hat, however, we have taken a less structured approach. We don't have any official policy for how much time each of our associates should spend "innovating." Rather, when deciding how to allocate resources for trying new things, we promote the idea that different people have earned different degrees of latitude to spend their time innovating. Many people frankly get little or none, while others, at the extreme, may get 100 percent of their time free to innovate. The most typical way is when someone works on a side project (maybe on Red Hat's time because they've been able to show their managers the value, or maybe on their own time until its value is evident), but later grows it into a full-time gig.

We encourage this kind of approach for a specific reason: we want the people who have proven to be great innovators to spend all of their time innovating, not just 20 percent of it. For example, consider how one top developer, Gavin King, essentially went off on his own, without any direction from above, to develop a new programming language called Ceylon. King, who joined Red Hat when his former employer, JBoss, was acquired in 2006, had grown frustrated with the limitations of Java, a programming language released by Sun Microsystems in 1995 that made it possible for internet software programs to run on just about any kind of computer operating system. While Java remains extremely popular and useful, King saw a need to update its capabilities, especially in developing new user interfaces. That's exactly what he and a community of other developers he recruited to help him accomplished. Ceylon is just one example of the innovative and game-changing products that have come from the R&D efforts of our top programmers. While we don't know how commercially successful Ceylon will be down the road, the key point is, as we like to put it, we don't sedate our rock stars.

Similarly, the associates at W. L. Gore also have the freedom to pursue projects that match up with their skills and passion. As the authors of *The Great Workplace* put it, "Gore associates have the freedom and the responsibility to increase their contributions while building their expertise. While formal classes and performance discussions are held, associates are free to innovate in their career paths at Gore as much as they innovate in product development."[10] According to Gary Hamel, at Gore, "the focus is on giving product champions time to experiment and learn, and taking small risks rather than betting the ranch too early. It's a way to organize for innovation, rather than plan for innovation, with a long-term view."[11]

At Red Hat, we encourage associates to work on what interests them and then watch what happens when they put their energy and talent into their work, whatever their role. "In any job, there are those projects that look like some small, boring things to check the box on," says Rebecca Fernandez. "But at Red Hat, there are so many opportunities for you to rethink those kinds of projects and say, 'No, this is bigger than what you're suggesting, there's an opportunity here to do something more valuable,' and maybe take that project in an entirely different and better direction." That kind of meritocratic freedom to run with your ideas is where some of our best work happens, and is some of the most gratifying.

Rather than impose a strategic or operational direction from above, Red Hat allows star associates to determine the best route forward. That helps explain why the adage, "Ask for forgiveness, not permission," is often repeated, whether it applies to an unofficial skunk works project or not.

The flip side of this approach would be a more democratic culture, where everyone is entitled to the same rights and opportunities.

While this might sound good on paper, the results simply don't add up. Given the competitive nature of our market, for instance, we as a company simply cannot afford to have one-fifth of our associates' time spent on efforts that might not have any positive return on that massive investment. Sure, we'd be successful now and again, assuming we had done our job in hiring talented and motivated individuals. But we've found that it's far more fruitful to let folks like Gavin King do what they do best with their time—to run with many ideas even as they do their regular work—and that's something they earn by delivering great results.

There are many great examples beyond the work Red Hat does on software. One is the contact strategy and customer reference team, which works with our customers to provide everything from case studies and speakers at a user conference, to references, quotes, and testimonials for the media and sales prospects (among other contributions). The contact strategy and customer reference team evolved from an idea hatched by Red Hatter Kathryn Poole.

A few years ago, Poole, who was working on the Red Hat public relations team, found that she was fielding more and more requests from the sales team or the media to talk to customers. This was creating confusion for customers, who sometimes had multiple requests from different Red Hat associates to deal with, and creating internal conflict among Red Hatters, who wanted to protect those relationships.

Poole saw an opportunity to simplify those dynamics. She suggested to her manager at the time, Leigh Day, that she could create a new position for herself where she would serve both the company and the customers by becoming a liaison. "I thought it would be great to have a program that created a more formalized approach to how we dealt with our customers and made sure we honored them for their contributions," Poole told me. "We wanted to make them IT heroes."

In the true spirit of the open organization, Day told Poole to go for it. She has since grown the program to include three other full-time associates and become an integral component of how Red Hat interacts with customers worldwide. "One of the cool things about working for Red Hat is that we give people enough leeway to go out and find your own role," says Poole. "You get to design your own destiny. Nobody is going to create your career path for you, which makes some people uncomfortable. But if you can prove that you're providing value, then people want to help you achieve success with it rather than seeing it as some kind of a land grab."

Examples like this aren't "nice to haves" at Red Hat. We rely on this type of self-direction as a key component of the management system. We use individual initiative and freedom to replace many of the typical management processes that would have identified this need, built the business case, justified it in the planning and budget processes, and ultimately implemented it. Yes, we do sometimes create business cases and we certainly have a budgeting process, but those are less onerous than is typical at companies of similar size and are designed to complement, not replace, the natural innovation coming from associates.

This example also illustrates the important role that leaders play in this system. Managers help foster an environment where associates feel comfortable asking to build something new. They create the space for people to operate. Those are the traits that leaders must exhibit to successfully lead open organizations.

Organizing for Success

You might infer that managers are less important in a meritocracy than in a hierarchical organization because they make fewer direct decisions. Nothing could be further from the truth. Our managers play a vital role in building, supporting, and moderating the meritocracy. Finding that balance between supporting it and, at the same time, leaving things alone is critical. To support the growth of a meritocracy, for example, you'll need tools like memo-list that give a voice to all employees, so they can begin to build influence among their peers. As a leader or manager, you'll also need to keep your ears open to not simply the loudest voices, but the ones that carry the most sway.

What you don't want to do, however, is try to squash the organic nature of how the meritocracy might self-organize. All too often, companies, especially fast-growth or larger organizations, buy into the idea that they have to systematize and sanitize their organizational culture to help gain control. But, by doing so, they also begin to make excuses and create shortcuts for their underachievers—an idea that runs counter to everything a meritocracy stands for.

As the president and CEO of a fast-growing, publicly traded company, I understand the difficulty of this pull to control things. I've realized though that I have had to establish my own reputation as well, which has pushed me to be a better listener and leader. I know that I don't have all the answers for where the company or its technology needs to head into the future. But I also know that I will do my best to empower the most innovative associates to help me map that road ahead. Again, it's not always a neat, pretty, or efficient process, but it works.

While we've taken the notion of a meritocracy to an extreme at Red Hat, it's not rocket science. Any leader at any company can improve his or her organization's performance by simply engaging the thermostats. Most people know who the thought leaders are. Ask around your own organization, and just about anyone can tell you who the thermostats are. The key for you as a leader and an organization, however, is to think about how to best use these people, regardless of their role in the company, to help drive innovation forward. Sometimes that can mean creating a physical atmosphere to promote that kind of mind-set.

For example, the financial services firm Edward Jones, which has more than eleven thousand locations and some 7 million clients, ditched its system of formal job descriptions in favor of what it calls "responsibility statements" that the company's associates write themselves. The associates define their own jobs. While I think some readers might be saying that's akin to turning the zoo over to the animals, it's actually an effective strategy in which the associates define their goals and how to measure the results they will attain to reach those goals. It's not about describing daily activities as much as giving the associates control over their own career paths. "We don't tell associates exactly what they have to do, when they have to do it, or how they have to do it," said Jim Weddle, the firm's managing partner. "With responsibility-based management, decisions are made by the people who are the experts because they are the ones doing the work. It makes us more nimble, more able to make good decisions quickly. We take more satisfaction for our work because we've assumed responsibility for it."[12]

Similarly, I recently spoke with a senior executive at a large insurance company. In order to foster innovation, he had selected teams to innovate on specific areas of the business. One team member he chose was a security guard at one of the company's facilities. While he might seem an odd choice, that security guard is one of the company's largest patent holders. Thermostats are everywhere in your organization: ignore them at your peril.

The Path to Earning Respect as a Leader

How would you be perceived in your own organization's meritocracy? Ask yourself if you command respect because people have to respect you or, rather, because you've truly earned respect. Many people aspire to titles because that forces others to respect them. But, to me, this is the lowest form of respect, especially if the person you're receiving respect from is more junior than you or works at a lower rung in the bureaucracy. Respect has to be earned. It's not about a title.

When people respect you only because of your authority, they will give you the minimum effort. Some incredibly brilliant people have earned respect because they are so smart, but most people aren't incredibly brilliant. So how do you go about it? There are three ways:

1. *Show passion for the purpose of your organization and constantly drive interest in it.* People are drawn to and generally want to follow passionate people. At Red Hat, that means being passionate about open source.

2. *Demonstrate confidence.* Many people in positions of authority don't show confidence well, especially with their team. It's one thing to convey confidence to your own boss, but it's just as important to share that same confidence with those who report to you.

3. *Engage your people.* Trust has to be earned, and it's not enough to call a meeting and tell people what to do and then retreat behind your own closed door. You also need to be open about your weaknesses and ask the team to help you address them. Nobody expects perfection, so don't hold your cards too close; get your team to work with you.

As a leader, it's so easy to surround yourself with people who think exactly the same way that you do, or at least who tell you what you want to hear. Those people are everywhere, and they're often the first to speak up. But if you really want to learn, seek out those people who present a divergent viewpoint and who will tell you what you need to hear, even when it's not easy.

Certainly, joining Red Hat posed a challenge for me. While I had a degree in computer science, I had no background in enterprise IT. In a very open, interactive culture like Red Hat's, there was no way for me to fake it. However, I found that being very open about the things I did not know actually had the opposite effect than I would have thought. It helped me build credibility. My team learned that I wouldn't feign knowledge where I did not have it and therefore was more likely to give me the benefit of the doubt when I did talk confidently. No one expects leaders to know everything all the time, but we do expect our leaders to be truthful and forthright.

Still a Work in Progress

At Red Hat, one of the greatest insults or blows to your ego comes when you put something on one of the internal discussion threads and receive nothing back—neither positive nor negative. "That's the worst outcome, truly," Kim Jokisch, director of Red Hat's employment branding and communications team, told me. "That means they're likely ignoring it, which means you've failed in some way."

Even so, the goal is not simply to generate posts and responses. That's not what builds your credibility. Rather, it's all about your true purpose. "People smell out intention around here," says Emily Stancil Martinez, a member of Red Hat's corporate communications team. "If your intention is just to stick your nose into every little thing so you can be front and center, people see it and will take note. But if you are thoughtful when you weigh in, in order to make a real contribution for the greater good, that's what truly builds your credibility and raises your profile."

But having the patience to build up that level of credibility can be frustrating to someone who joins the team. A new hire—especially someone who hasn't already built a reputation in the open source community—simply won't have the same level of influence as, say, Máirín Duffy or Thomas Cameron. It doesn't always seem fair, and some good ideas are likely never heard as a result. An enthusiastic new hire may join the company with the thought that his ideas will be heard equally, only to fall into a rut when he feels as if his good ideas are ignored. That can quickly lead to a disengaged employee who either leaves the company or, worse, becomes a cultural nay-sayer. Part of the solution is to set expectations so people know that earning a reputation takes time and hard work. It's as if you want to sell something on a site like eBay: without any history or reputation score, you can find it far harder to locate buyers interested in what you're selling. That takes time, patience, and a commitment to working at building your reputation, which isn't something every-one enjoys doing. The upside of this kind of culture far outweighs any downside. The system is a work in progress, but is still a system that is light years ahead of the conventional organization approach.

Jim's Leadership Tips

1. ***Don't use phrases like "the boss wants it this way" or rely on hierarchical name dropping.*** While that may get things done in the short term, it can curtail discussion that's core to building a meritocracy.

2. ***Publicly recognize a great effort or contribution.*** It can be a simple thank-you e-mail in which you copy the whole team.

3. ***Consider whether your influence comes from your position in the hierarchy (or access to privileged information), or whether it truly comes from respect that you have earned.*** If it is the former, start working on the latter.

4. ***Proactively ask for feedback and ideas on a specific topic.*** You must respond to them all, but implement only the good ones. And don't just take the best ideas and move on; take every opportunity to reinforce the spirit of meritocracy by giving credit where it's due.

5. ***Reward a high-performing member of your team with an interesting assignment, even if it is not in his or her usual area.***

5

Letting the Sparks Fly

Early on in my Red Hat career, I was working from home one day after a doctor's appointment. I had a phone meeting with Paul Cormier, Red Hat's president of products and technologies. Cormier and I discussed a variety of issues, as we always do, and then eventually wrapped up our talk. My wife, who was at home during the call, came over and asked, "Oh my gosh, what's wrong? It sounds like you just had a huge fight!" This caught me by surprise. I said, "No, we didn't. We were just debating something and trying to find a solution."

What I realized then was that many of our discussions at Red Hat involve heated and passionate debate, something that rarely happened in my earlier jobs. Certainly, most interactions are not as heated as my discussion with Cormier was that day—he and I have developed our own norms over the years—but Red Hat associates' passion for the business and comfort with speaking our minds make the average interaction much more frank than I've seen at conventional organizations. In my experience, if someone disagreed with something you said in a meeting, he would rarely confront you about it, and certainly not in Red Hat's open and unvarnished way, especially to dare questioning someone higher up on the corporate hierarchy.

Luckily, I started my career in what I would characterize as an intellectual meritocracy. At BCG, a professional services firm with many bright, motivated people where the product was our thoughts and ideas, we had many spirited, free-flowing debates. While the partners were clearly in charge, there was a deep cultural ethos of seeking truth and give-and-take. Case teams at BCG were encouraged to have healthy debates, which often lasted late into the night. I loved it. But I also knew that when I left to join the corporate world, I would have to leave this behind. That type of debate is rare across levels in a conventional organization.

When I got to Red Hat, though, I quickly learned that you can't get the best creativity, initiative, or effort from the members of an open organization by saying, "Go do this." The best ideas happen when teams hash things out. Engineers at Red Hat have publicly challenged my decisions. That would never have happened at Delta. These challenges are typically quite respectful and well thought out, and rarely cross the line. But public, open disagreement is part of how Red Hat works; I'm convinced that we get better answers as a result. I love working, debating, and sometimes arguing with people to solve hard, complex issues. I love to argue—not maliciously—but in a healthy way in which both sides are heard. I love to stir up a good debate and sometimes think of myself as Red Hat's head debater. When you start a conversation, you're more likely to find better solutions. I didn't bring this component of our culture to Red Hat; it was already there, but I do feel right at home with it. As the legendary management guru Peter Drucker so aptly put it, "The only way to discover your strengths is through feedback analysis."[1]

At Red Hat, even our values—freedom, courage, commitment, and accountability—intentionally create a degree of tension (see figure 5-1). These four values, which the company chose in 2002, well before I joined the team in 2008, still resonate with everything we do today. This is true in large part because they weren't handed down from executives after returning from a weekend retreat. Red Hatters themselves chose them and have since embedded them into the fabric of the corporate culture. And those values require thought. Most companies' values are decidedly noncontroversial. Our values, on the other hand, address our aspirations—what we believe in. And we accept that those things can, at times, be in conflict. They therefore require constant balance.

Our values, usually represented as balls on a scale to show that balance, also illustrate how the debates in a highly collaborative culture can, in fact, be quite productive, despite "letting the sparks fly." Think about how freedom, for example, can directly oppose accountability or commitment. People might ask, if freedom is a value, what's to stop someone from declaring he has the freedom to not show up for work? But freedom is balanced out by another value—accountability. People do have a great deal of freedom at Red Hat, but when we are at our best, this freedom is kept in check

FIGURE 5-1

Red Hat's four values

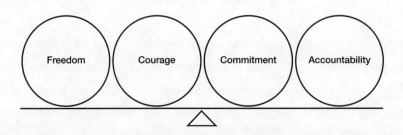

Freedom   Courage   Commitment   Accountability

by accountability—to each other, to our partners and customers, and to our shareholders.

As an organization, we're like a ship that rights itself when we lean too heavily in the direction of any one of the four values. People who naturally gravitate toward freedom or courage don't find it easy to work with those who lean more heavily toward accountability or commitment. That inherent tension and conflict between our values is part of why they're so compelling to our associates. Red Hatters continually experience this push and pull within the company. The willingness to address tension is built deep into our corporate DNA.

At Red Hat, solving problems head-on is a big part of the culture. We're in the business of working with communities, customers, and partners to solve complex IT challenges (think of the cloud and big data). While we don't necessarily argue for argument's sake, we can be really passionate about getting things right. Many see a highly collaborative culture as a supportive, positive environment where people encourage each other with positive reinforcement. Actually, Red Hat is anything but that. It is very supportive and collaborative, but in a very different way. We debate, we argue, and we complain. In many ways, it can seem harsh. But iron sharpens iron, and we've come to embrace the notion of letting the sparks fly.

Beyond Brainstorming

When people envision what good collaboration looks like, most picture classic brainstorming techniques in which positive reinforcement is used to encourage participation. Brainstorming was originally conceived by famed ad man Alex Osborn, founder of the advertising agency BBDO; the idea behind it was to use positive reinforcement and feedback to stimulate people's creativity—"there is no such thing as a bad idea"—a technique that has been widely employed since Osborn laid out the ground rules in his 1948 book, *Your Creative Power.*

Osborn's technique has been challenged in recent years. For instance, in a 2003 study, Charlan Nemeth, a professor of psychology at the University of California, Berkeley, found that emphasizing the "debate condition," in which people are encouraged to challenge and debate each other's ideas, actually generates substantially more new ideas than Osborn's approach. As recounted in a *New Yorker* article titled, "Groupthink: The Brainstorming Myth," Nemeth said:

> *While the instruction "Do not criticize" is often cited as the important instruction in brainstorming, this appears to be a counterproductive strategy. Our findings show that debate and criticism do not inhibit ideas but, rather, stimulate them relative to every other condition . . . There's this Pollyannaish notion that the most important thing to do when working together is stay positive and get along, to not hurt anyone's feelings. Well, that's just wrong. Maybe debate is going to be less pleasant, but it will always be more productive. True creativity requires some trade-offs.*[2]

Similarly, in his book, *59 Seconds: Think a Little, Change a Lot*, psychologist Richard Wiseman reached the conclusion that simply gathering a group of people together does not ensure that they'll reach creative conclusions. He writes: "When strong-willed people lead group discussion, they can pressure others into conforming, can encourage self-censorship, and can create an illusion of unanimity. Two heads are not necessarily better than one. More than fifty years of research suggest that irrational thinking occurs when people try to reach decisions in groups, and this can lead to a polarization of opinions and a highly biased assessment of a situation."[3]

One term we often hear is *groupthink*, coined by William H. Whyte, author of *The Organization Man*, in a 1952 issue of *Fortune*. The idea is that when a group of people work together, they tend to want to reach some kind of harmony and to minimize conflict, which so often leads to terrible and even tragic results. James Surowiecki tackles this subject in his now famous book, *The Wisdom of Crowds*, in which he discusses the research done by the Yale University psychologist Irving Janis to understand how groupthink was responsible for the poor decision making leading up to events like the attack on Pearl Harbor and the Bay of Pigs invasion. Surowiecki writes: "Homogeneous groups become more cohesive more easily than diverse groups, and as they become more cohesive they become more dependent on the group, more isolated from outside opinions, and therefore more convinced that the group's judgment on important issues must be right. These kinds of groups, Janis suggested, share an illusion of invulnerability, a willingness to rationalize away counterarguments to the group's position, and a conviction that dissent is not useful."[4] In other words, there's almost a constant bias for us to go along with the will of the crowd—to please others and fit in, regardless of whether we truly agree with the consensus.

That's where the power of what the authors of *Collective Genius* call "creative abrasion," which they define as something that involves some level of conflict—a disagreement, contention, or argument— that works best when it's practiced within a community that has a shared purpose, shared values, and rules of engagement that help keep the conflict productive rather than destructive.[5] The film studio Pixar is a big believer in the power of such creative abrasion, and its executives credit open debates within the ranks of their creative people for pushing the boundaries of what was possible for animated movies such as *Toy Story*, *A Bug's Life*, *Cars*, and *Up*. "There is no doubt that our decision-making is better if we are able to draw on the collective knowledge and unvarnished opinions of the group," said Ed Catmull, one of Pixar's cofounders, who strongly believes in the value of "candor"—meaning forthrightness or frankness—when working through opportunities and challenges. Pixar has even created an organizational group called the "Brain Trust" whose function is to get candid feedback on whatever movies the studio happens to be working on. "A hallmark of a healthy creative culture is that its people feel free to share ideas, opinions, and criticisms," Catmull said. "Lack of candor, if unchecked, ultimately leads to dysfunctional environments."[6]

Similarly, John Seely Brown, the former head of Xerox PARC, once said, "Breakthroughs often appear in the white space between crafts. These crafts start to collide, and in that collision radically new things start to happen."[7] Bill Coughran, a former senior vice president of engineering, infrastructure group at Google, was quoted as saying: "Managing tensions in the organization is an ongoing issue . . . You don't want an organization that just salutes and does what you say. You want an organization that argues with you. And so you want to nurture the bottoms up, but you've got to be careful that you don't degenerate into chaos."[8]

An interesting characteristic of open source software communities is that, as a whole, they tend to embrace the approach championed by Nemeth and others who see the value in stirring the pot and dissenting from the crowd. Online forums and chat rooms are often filled with spirited and sometimes caustic back-and-forth debates about everything from how best to fix a software bug to what new features to consider in a subsequent release. Usually, there is a first phase of discussions in which new ideas are posited and collected, but there is always a subsequent round of critical analysis. While anyone may have the ability to wade into these debates, in doing so, they should be prepared to defend their position with every ounce of their ability. Unpopular ideas will be, at best, shot down and, at worst, ridiculed.

For example, even Linus Torvalds, founder of the Linux operating system, voices his disagreement with proposed changes to the code on message boards. In one case, he and David Howells, one of Red Hat's lead developers, got into a heated discussion on the Linux Kernel Mailing List about the merit of a change in the code Red Hat was asking for, which would help our clients with security. In response to a request from Howells, Torvalds wrote back:

> *Quite frankly, this is [bleeping] moronic. The whole thing seems to be designed around stupid interfaces, for completely moronic reasons. Why should we do this? I already dislike our existing X.509 parser. And this makes the idiotic complicated interfaces, and now it goes up to 11. Linus*[9]

Technical details aside, Torvalds went on to say a few more choice things in a subsequent note that I won't get into here. That conversation got so loud that even the *Wall Street Journal* covered it. "An argument between software engineers working for open source distributor Red Hat Inc. and Linux founder Linus Torvalds embodies the tension between pragmatists and idealists that exists in almost every business, and underlies many decisions made not only in building software, but involving just about any product that's brought to market," wrote Michael Hickins in an article with the headline: "Linux Throw-Down Sheds Light on 'Moronic' Software Processes."[10]

Hickins frames the argument by showing how, in most proprietary software companies, there is no public debate about what new features or changes the company might be working on. When the product is ready, the company simply ships it out to customers and moves on. With Linux, however, there is an almost constant debate about what changes might be needed and—most importantly—why they're needed. That, of course, makes the whole process a lot messier and more time consuming. As Hickins writes: "Keeping those arguments behind closed doors allows vendors of proprietary software to ship products more quickly than purists might like, even if it means having to patch or upgrade the software later. Hashing out arguments out in the open helps ensure software purists have their say and, in many cases, their way."[11]

My point is that this is the culture that Red Hat has grown out of. At the beginning, the company was really just a bunch of developers and hackers who embraced the whole idea of working in the spirit of open source. That meant engaging in heated debates about, well, just about everything. But as the company has grown, it has become much more than just a group of coders. People work in everything from marketing and human resources to finance. Yet, as we've grown up, we've kept that spirit of collaboration and debate alive so that it affects just about every decision we make as a company.

I am certainly not advocating that the Linux community's brash style is generally appropriate. It has taken the model to an extreme. In fact, Red Hat actively works to ensure that open source communities welcome diverse people and thoughts. We need to navigate a tightrope between providing honest and unvarnished feedback without crossing the line to be offensive. Most people are naturally nice. We would much rather compliment than criticize. Others even avoid conflict. But a key theme throughout this book is that leaders must often foster and encourage debate. If you don't debate things and solicit feedback, that's a problem. If you like top-down order and structure in discussions, the kind of chaotic culture we have built at Red Hat won't appeal to you.

It takes time to get used to our open, frank style of debate. But for some of our developers—in particular, those who have spent years in their open source communities—we've actually had to work to find a compromise. We've learned to embrace the phrase, "You aren't your code," which is used in the open source world to emphasize that just because someone is criticizing what you've done, it doesn't mean they are criticizing you personally. We have worked hard so people don't let their feelings get hurt when someone disagrees with their idea; those are two separate things. They need to be able to remove themselves from their work to look at it objectively. But it's a work in progress. We want to make sure that we keep our edge without alienating others who join our mission.

Adopting a New Mind-Set

During Delta's bankruptcy restructuring, I worked with a number of people whose full-time jobs are to help distressed companies. These bankers and lawyers specialize in bankruptcies and out of court debt restructurings. I learned that they often use the expression "terminally nice" to describe clients. They often see companies with cultures that avoid conflict, so they never have frank, unpleasant conversations that are needed. These companies end up in real trouble because the cultures never initiate the difficult conversations that drive superior performance.

Everyone knows the expression "the elephant in the room" (or some variant of it). In other words, everyone knows what the real issue is, but no one wants to raise and discuss it, because it's personally painful and full of conflict. One of the biggest threats any executive faces is the notion that he or she is only hearing the good stuff about the business. People generally want to please, so it can be a challenge to encourage them to deliver the bad along with the good. Open organizations adopt an open mind-set so they can encourage everyone to speak up and share insights. While most companies fortunately don't reach the point of being "terminally nice," many never reach their full potential because they don't address the hard issues. In most conventional organizations, the biggest clue that there is disagreement among the team is that nobody says anything at all. That's why encouraging dissenting opinions is so critical to success in making the culture in an open organization come together.

The team at W. L. Gore apparently agrees with this as well. The company's CEO, Terri Kelly, has said that a big part of her job is getting out and talking to her associates in person, sometimes as many as a hundred to two hundred at a time. As part of those town hall–style talks, Kelly encourages her team to tell her how to truly stoke two-way communications throughout the organization. As one associate says, it's an important part of their culture: "I can sit in a room with Terri Kelly and really battle out a difference of opinion and feel no fear of repercussion as a result of that kind of behavior. In fact, it's the expected behavior. We have the opportunity to connect whenever we need to connect to take on whatever might be the issue or the opportunity of the day."[12]

At Red Hat meetings, people might actually go out of their way to argue a point. Our meetings have more words spoken per minute than in any other company out there, not because people are trying to be difficult, but because they are so passionate. They like to push the discussion further than it might go to take another side of the argument.

For example, soon after I joined Red Hat, we made a very important (and strategic) technology decision in our virtualization business when we purchased Qumranet—a story I told in chapter 3. In the same spirit of trying to build engagement from the beginning, a number of our top technical people participated in an evaluation process to help us make the best possible choice when we made that acquisition.

But even after we made our decision, one of the engineers called me out in front of the group—which included his boss, his boss's boss, and more—letting me know that he thought we were making the wrong choice. He also went to great lengths to explain why. While I thanked him for his input—he did make many valid arguments—I continued to believe we were on the right path. Meanwhile, as he was talking, I kept looking at his boss and his boss's boss to see how they were reacting to this engineer speaking up as he was. This kind of thing never happened at Delta. If it had, people would have been turning purple with rage. An unwritten workplace rule was you didn't call out your boss—let alone your boss's boss—in front of their boss. The whole scene only added to my sense that this company was chaotic.

But that engineer's words never left me. It also soon became clear that he was right—the decision we made just wasn't the best one for Red Hat. So we made a major about-face when it came to the technology. It was costly and time consuming, but it was the better decision. I share this story not to be cavalier about the significant financial investments we made. Rather, I'd like to stress that I couldn't let my ego—or the fact that we had been wrong—get in the way of making the best possible decisions for the company. Building an open organization with a participatory culture like Red Hat's is all about encouraging debate and celebrating the best ideas, regardless of who or where they come from. It's not an easy thing to do, but it's the right thing if you want to build a more engaged, collaborative, and innovative workforce.

What can seem harsh at times is that no matter what you bring up, you can expect someone to challenge you. The beauty of this approach is that you will always have multiple views from different people to use as you form your own opinions. If, by contrast, the goal is for everyone in a meeting to be nice to each other and every idea is treated as a good one, you can end up with results nobody is pleased with. A famous quote from Sir Alec Issigonis frames it: "A camel is a horse designed by committee." In other words, when you try to please everyone, you often wind up incorporating elements that nobody wants or needs. When you weave healthy debate and honesty into a conversation, though, your results can be fundamentally different.

For instance, when I go on sales calls with reps from Red Hat and ask them, "How are things?" I rarely get a response like, "Everything is fine." What I hear instead is a litany of issues about what the reps think we could be doing better or what problems they are facing and what they think they need to do in order to overcome them. They unload on me. That's the kind of interaction that is the opposite of being terminally nice, and it means I'm hearing what's really going on in the business. While it would certainly be easier to hear "everything is great," I know ultimately we perform better as a company because we don't take the easy way out.

Google relies on something called "Google Ideas," a web-based forum where employees regularly submit ideas on everything from product improvements to making the company a better place to work. The rest of the Google team can then weigh in with opinions on those ideas using a zero- to five-point scale. Google's management team pays close attention to the activity on the ideas site to see which ones are trending and should perhaps be escalated to other communication levels in the company, say, by including it in a companywide e-mail discussion. What makes this kind of forum so valuable is that every employee at Google has a way to collect feedback—both objective and admittedly subjective—from peers with the ultimate goal of having the best ideas bubble up to the top.[13]

At Red Hat, as I mentioned earlier, we rely heavily on forums like memo-list to facilitate conversations on everything from opinions on new technology to discussing the latest scuttlebutt on our competitors. To make our system of letting the sparks fly work, though, as a leader in the organization, I can't moderate such discussions by deleting or reprimanding or setting rules. That would squash the conversation. I encourage people to constructively criticize, because most people won't. Now and then, there's a post that says something obnoxious, but those get quickly shouted down. The real problem is getting people who are genuinely nice to say something that might be harsh. I have to ask people, "What did you mean by that?" Sometimes people on a mailing list might say an idea is stupid, even pointing out everything that's wrong with one of my ideas. But that's OK. It's how you get to the best ideas, and it frees your organization from the dangers of terminal niceness.

For example, Vineet Nayar, the CEO who helped lead a dramatic turnaround at HCL Technologies, an information technology consulting company based in India, started an internal blog he calls "My Problems," in which he posts the strategic problems he's working on to collect feedback and ideas from anyone in the company willing to share thoughts. As the authors of *Conscious Capitalism* write, this forum gives Nayar "access to a huge amount of fresh thinking about such questions, and it also encourages more people to think more broadly and strategically about the business."[14]

The key is to strive to find the balance between shutting down debate when posts become caustic, while also continuing to push people to give you the kind of frank feedback you're looking for. This is where we rely heavily on our culture of 360-degree accountability and peer-to-peer management. The worst thing we could do as an organization is make it seem as if the CEO and management team are somehow trying to shut people up, even if they might be out of line. The job for the crowd is to help self-police our e-mail lists. At the same time, we have to encourage people to participate, but we can't then say every idea is great. That's what can be difficult for some people to adapt to.

Growing a Thick Skin

The feedback from sharing new ideas at Red Hat can sometimes feel blunt and brutally honest, regardless of who originated the idea. "People are passionate about the company and what we do," Máirín Duffy, a user-interface designer, told me. "When people interpret something as going against the company's core values, they feel threatened, and that is when the sparks really fly." That means that memo-list can be a somewhat dangerous place if Red Hatters don't take the time to think before they write. To work in such an environment, therefore, people need a pretty thick skin. Given that the back-and-forth can be challenging, many newcomers to the company are left to wonder, "You call this collaboration?" This approach to generating and sharing new ideas may be difficult—it certainly requires lots of effort—but it works. And that's why we make letting the sparks fly such a clear component of our corporate culture, while also recognizing that it takes some time to adjust to.

For example, Kim Jokisch, director of Red Hat's employment branding team, left a job at The Body Shop to join Red Hat back in 2002. The Body Shop, founded by Anita Roddick, was one of the pioneering companies in creating natural cosmetic products. It was, as Jokisch puts it, a "good news kind of business," and the people who worked there felt as if they were making a difference in the world. But it was still a conventional organization. When Jokisch got to Red Hat, she felt the difference in culture immediately. While there was a similar passion for making the world a better place, there was also an edge she wasn't used to, something that was driven home when she began rolling out new programs such as a performance management system and a more formalized approach to interviewing candidates.

"We were starting to hire a lot more people, and we needed to formalize our processes," Jokisch told me. "We wanted to institute behavioral-based systems, rather than something that was more ad hoc. So, I researched the best programs we could put in place, got certified, and then traveled around the globe, training our managers and people on how to use them."

That's just about when the sparks began to fly. "I was really surprised by the amount of pushback I got, where people all over the company said things like, 'This will take too much time,' or 'What do you mean I can't ask that?'" said Jokisch, who had been doing such training for about ten years before she got to Red Hat. "I began thinking, 'What have I done? I left this great job where there was always positive feedback on everything you did. Now I am being challenged every step of the way. It often felt like I had to justify everything I did."

To her credit, Jokisch recognized that feedback of any kind should be considered a gift, even if it's painful at first. She realized that she needed to engage people in the process and collaborate to find the best solution, rather than going off on her own and forcing a particular solution.

The open communication channels at Red Hat can sometimes seem like, according to one Red Hatter, "a pool full of piranhas." But the sharing of feelings and opinions is ultimately a positive thing because it reinforces that anyone can have a say, which leads to increased engagement. "What I quickly realized was that even harsh feedback makes you smarter and better at your job because it helps you think of things from different angles," Jokisch told me. "To be successful, then, you really have to check your ego at the door and recognize that there are a lot of other smart people working here and that by getting their feedback and point of view, you're going to be better at what you do."

While developing a thick skin is a prerequisite for success at Red Hat, everyone also needs to recognize, respect, and have flexibility in understanding and engaging with the different cultures within the company. As things have changed over time, not all areas of the company are the same. The engineers, for example, who work more closely with open source communities, tend to be much harsher in sharing their feedback than are other teams. We've discussed internally how best to handle those kinds of differences and concluded that we don't want to have a single overriding culture. It can be OK to have differences in cultural areas as long as everyone believes we are all working for better outcomes throughout the organization. People have different personalities and priorities; they think and speak out in different ways. These differences can make letting the sparks fly even more challenging. But you don't want to strip away differences in trying to get to consensus, because that can lead to groupthink, poor decisions, and stalled innovation. People must be encouraged to speak up, in their own distinct ways, and rewarded when they do.

"It's not just debate though—it's action, too," Duffy told me. "Talk without action isn't regarded very highly. For example, if you complain about a piece of software we make not doing something you think it should, you're going to be regarded as noise unless you step up and actually write some code to prototype the idea. Or, if you complain that the company uses some piece of software that isn't good, you better back up your complaint with some suggestions for better things, or you will be regarded as just adding noise."

The Leader's Role: Knocking Down Barriers to Collaboration

Technology companies are known for casual dress. You can walk the streets of Palo Alto past the cafés and restaurants for hours and never see a tie. But many of the same technology companies that employ these folks have rigid hierarchies that would match anything a military academy can muster. Steve Jobs dressed casually, but there was no question who was in charge at Apple. At Red Hat, we embrace informality in myriad ways, not because we like to be comfortable in what we wear or that we wouldn't like couches in the executive suite, but because we've learned that to truly encourage dialogue and debate across the company, we have to break down any semblance of an "us and them" culture.

In conventional hierarchical organizations, the trappings of power can actually play a constructive role. They are visual cues for people's positions in the organization. Since decision rights correlate to level, having visible ways to show differences in position can be helpful. When I worked at Delta, wearing a suit and tie was a measure of rank in the corporate hierarchy. As soon as you were promoted to vice president, you received a sticker for your car that corresponded with your own personal parking space with your name on it. Every day when I drove in, the guards at the gate would salute me and call me "sir."

That helps explain why it took me a few months working at Red Hat before I noticed that I looked different from everyone, that the button-down shirt and pressed khakis I wore somehow set me apart, just as a suit and tie did at Delta. I was creating an invisible hierarchy without realizing it. The very next day, I came in wearing jeans and a casual shirt. It finally dawned on me that formality and visual cues could become barriers to collaboration. What I learned was that the people at Red Hat express themselves through their personalities, not their clothes or their rank. There are plenty of fancy cars in the Red Hat parking lot, but no one has an assigned space. Our associates recognize that promotions are more about validation of their value and hard work, not parking spaces and corner offices.

Something as simple as a T-shirt can break down barriers at Red Hat. Early on in my experience at Red Hat, my wife and kids were still living in Atlanta, so I was commuting back and forth on the weekends until we settled in Raleigh. FUDCon, the Fedora Users and Developers Conference, a major open source software event, was being held on Saturday at the end of my first week. Kim Jokisch suggested that I stay the weekend so I could attend, since it would be a chance for me to connect with Red Hatters who had assembled for the event from all over. While I was clearly looking forward to seeing my family, I thought it was a great idea. I asked if I could get a Fedora T-shirt to wear to the event. The last thing I wanted was to show up looking like the typical corporate executive on a casual Friday. I didn't really have a grand motive for wearing the T-shirt. I just wanted to blend in. It took people a while to realize that this guy walking around in the Fedora T-shirt was the new CEO of Red Hat. I was surprised that people actually noticed. I heard about it several times in the weeks and months that followed and was later told that wearing the T-shirt bought me some added geek cred. The little symbolic things can truly make a real difference.

How we dress seems like a little thing, and many companies have adopted "business casual" policies. But to truly break down the barriers and get ideas freely flowing, things like how you dress need to reflect and reinforce your culture, not be at odds with it. The lesson, therefore, is about not just going through the motions but truly working to break down barriers. In other words, it's not really about the clothes.

Similarly, when I look back at my interview at Red Hat, which I talked about in chapter 1, when I wondered why I was the only one with cash in my wallet, I now realize that it never occurred to Matthew Szulik or Michael Cunningham to treat me any other way or to evaluate me based on my clothes. I wasn't special or privileged just because of my background or the job I was interviewing for (I would later learn that Szulik ran more than a few other recruits through a similar gauntlet). It was simply part of the company's culture in which meritocracy, not hierarchy, reigns supreme. If you like the accoutrements of power, Red Hat is most certainly not for you.

Breaking down hierarchies also includes removing all the forms of special treatments today's executives seem so entitled to, including titles. People at Red Hat care less about the outward signs of achievement and ladder climbing than in most conventional organizations. They keep their eyes on what they believe is truly important.

On my first full day on the job, I was directed to a cubicle that was just like everyone else's. Now, at the time of this writing, things have changed. Red Hat has moved its headquarters to a building in downtown Raleigh, where I have an office with a door. It's similar to the offices dozens of other people have—maybe I have a better view than some—but it's still far more mundane than the standard, conventional executive suites of the past.

This meritocratic mind-set pervades the entire company, which now has sales, development, and support offices worldwide. Part of Red Hat lore, for instance, is a picture that shows Brian Stevens, Red Hat's former executive vice president and chief technology officer

(CTO), with a bathroom plunger in his hand. As the story goes, Stevens—who had been with Red Hat for years and worked at the engineering office in Westford, Massachusetts—was famous for his hands-on attitude in tackling everything from cleaning the office toilets to lugging huge computer servers to trade shows across the country.

Of course, as CTO, Stevens could have ordered any number of people to tackle those tasks. And certainly, as CTO of a company with some seven thousand associates, he wouldn't technically have to. But Stevens understood what the Red Hat culture is really built on: merit, not titles. Just as any entrepreneur can't be too proud to tackle a job that needs to be done, so too do executives like Stevens and me have to be willing to roll up our sleeves and join the fight on the frontlines rather than sitting back to direct the battle from our posh corner offices.

Marco Bill-Peter, vice president of customer experience and engagement who heads up the global support organization, says that what enables people to thrive in Red Hat's culture is an informal personality. "The fact that we wear jeans isn't what makes us different from other companies out there," says Bill-Peter, who worked at tech giant Hewlett-Packard for thirteen years before joining Red Hat six years ago. "It's really about a willingness to put aside your ego while embracing openness and transparency. Titles don't mean a thing. That's why, for example, I don't print my title on any of my internal e-mails. Even when I introduce myself to other people in the company, I don't talk about how I'm a vice president. I usually just say, 'I'm the support dude.'"

Remember that someone wearing jeans and flip-flops can convey that she is still the boss. Just look at a company like Apple, where Steve Jobs was notorious for his casual dress, dating back to the company's earliest days. But, by most accounts, that didn't really make him more approachable; he was still at the center of Apple's "Cult of the CEO" kind of culture where every important decision went through him. In other words, the simple act of wearing jeans is not how you build engagement and break down hierarchies. It's the attitude adjustments that need to go along with it.

Why Healthy Debates Matter

The lack of frank dialogue is the single biggest controllable weakness that most companies impose upon themselves. Being nice and letting things slide add up over time to an organization that knows its core problems but is unable to act. While conflict avoidance isn't a direct outcome of a conventional organizational structure, hierarchies clearly tend to soften bad news when it's going up the chain. All but the brashest have difficulty asking questions in a rigid hierarchy. Finding ways to foster frank, productive feedback and debate can improve the performance of any organization. For a meritocracy, it's critical. As Ed Catmull of Pixar puts it:

> It isn't enough merely to be open to ideas from others. Engaging the collective brainpower of the people you work with is an active, ongoing process. As a manager, you must coax ideas out of your staff and constantly push them to contribute. There are many reasons why people aren't candid with one another in a work environment. Your job is to search for those reasons and then address them. Likewise, if someone disagrees with you, there is a reason. Our first job is to understand the reasoning behind their conclusions. If there is more truth in the hallways than in meetings, you have a problem.[15]

Not every organization is prepared to change its culture in a way that allows sparks to fly. As I've described, it's still a work in progress at Red Hat. Some people worry that my senior team is not functioning properly because of our open debates. I see it as the opposite. We have the open and frank debates we need. We continue to foster this attitude throughout the company, while also trying to find a balance between delivering good feedback and creating arguments just for the sake of having an argument. Some people say that they've waited to tackle new initiatives precisely because they weren't mentally ready to deal with the feedback and challenges they would inevitably endure, no matter how valuable that information might be. We're still learning.

Jim's Leadership Tips

1. ***Proactively invite feedback and then thank those who give it to you.*** Feedback is a gift. As a leader or manager, if you react defensively, you are unlikely to get that gift again.

2. ***Start a debate.*** If your organization isn't used to open, frank debate, start with easy topics. Make sure no one takes it personally.

3. ***If forums don't exist for healthy debate, create them.*** If you're a people manager, debating with your team is easy. If you're an individual contributor, find ways to initiate dialogue with others in the company.

4. ***Recognize the myriad barriers to frank dialogue.*** For example, never start a contentious conversation on opposite sides of a desk, and recognize that offices are home turf. Pick neutral places.

5. ***Does your organization avoid the "elephant in the room" conversations?*** If so, think about what role you can play to initiate those discussions.

PART THREE

WHAT

Setting Direction

6

Making Inclusive Decisions

The conventional approach to decision making centers around equipping the responsible person with the information needed to make an informed decision. It's about gathering facts and analysis and convening the appropriate team to give input. Companies often have entire strategic planning departments analyze, apply frameworks, and communicate recommendations. But in the end, based on that information and feedback, the responsible executive makes the decision.

The specific act of making a decision in a hierarchy can be very efficient. Only a single individual is needed to make the call. That can be a real benefit. However, as I described in chapter 3, there are myriad issues with this style of decision making. Appropriate information must flow unfiltered up the chain of command to the appropriate person in a timely way for him or her to make the right decision. The decision maker must have the appropriate context in which to best make the decision. That's a tall order. In this chapter,

I describe the other major issue with the conventional decision-making approach, namely, as a missed opportunity to build understanding, trust, and buy-in.

Making an executive decision by fiat is fast, but that's when the real hard work starts. Once a decision is made, it's now time to execute and bring about whatever changes were prescribed by that decision. Most major change projects fail. In an IBM study in 2008, researchers surveyed fifteen hundred executives in fifteen countries and found that some 60 percent of major projects fail to achieve their objectives.[1] Another study, conducted by the Standish Group, found that only 37 percent of projects are successfully implemented, with 21 percent of those failing completely, which leads to billions of dollars of lost resources and productivity.[2] Those sobering statistics are probably only going to get worse. The speed of business is accelerating, which means organizations can't afford to fail nearly 70 percent of the time.

In conventional organizations, frustrated executives—many of whom grumble that their people "don't want to change"—turn to consulting firms that have built entire practices around something known as "change management." Change management is the common name for the efforts required to get an organization to implement an initiative that requires people to change their behavior. Bigger decisions, ones that require significant change in what or how people work, are particularly difficult to bring about. The company needs to communicate the decision, convince people, and so on. In short, change management is hard.

These efforts, therefore, generally take a long time—possibly years—and are expensive in terms of resources required. Almost certainly, more time, energy, and money are spent on change management efforts than are spent on making the decision in the first place. Executives believe these massive efforts are required to overcome their organization's unwillingness to change. Instead, they should dig more deeply into how their own decision-making process may be causing the problem.

Firms like the clothing retailer Eileen Fisher, a global brand that emphasizes organically-grown fabrics for its clothes, have come to realize that the more people they include from their organization in their decisions, the more buy-in they'll receive as a result. Eileen Fisher created something it calls a "Leadership Forum," which originally consisted of twenty-one key leaders from across the company who met every three weeks or so to share information and make decisions and recommendations. The Eileen Fisher team evolved that system starting in 2007 when it began inviting people from nonsenior leadership positions to join the meetings as full participants, which helped both build relationships within the company and also reinforce the two-way culture it was trying to grow.[3]

After a few years at Red Hat, I also found that if you include the very people who will be affected in your decision-making process, change management becomes unimportant. You won't need to convince people, because they are involved in coming up with the answer. You'll be amazed at how the results differ.

The Power of Including Others

Marriott International, which began as a root beer stand in 1927 and now has more than thirty-seven hundred hotels in seventy-four countries, credits its core values—"Putting people first, pursuing excellence, embracing change, acting with integrity, and serving our world"—for driving that kind of sustaining growth and for extensive recognition for its culture and treatment of employees.[4] In an interview, J. W. Marriott Jr., former CEO of the company, discussed witnessing firsthand how former president Dwight Eisenhower seemed to thrive on including the opinions of others in making decisions. Marriott said that affected how he made decisions in his own company: "I tried to adopt that style of management as I progressed in life, by asking my people, 'What do you think?' Now, I didn't always go with what they thought. But I felt that if I included them in the decision-making process, and asked them what they thought, and I listened to what they had to say and considered it, they usually got on board because they knew they'd been respected and heard, even if I went in a different direction than what they were recommending."[5]

Similarly, Red Hat has taught me the power of inclusiveness to the extreme. I have learned the value of getting associates involved in creating the solutions rather than just sharing the decisions with them afterward. Go out and talk to the people with whom you work. By using technology as an ally, you can reach out to far more people in the organization that can fit in any one meeting room. When you do, be open, honest, and frank. One of the worst sins I can commit, as a leader at Red Hat, is to surprise the organization with a decision I make. People at Red Hat are generally happy—morale scores are very high—precisely because we make sure everyone who works here knows his or her role in tackling the mission.

Millennials, folks born between 1980 and 2000, have been discussed ad nauseam in the mainstream business literature. The general conclusion is that this generation is less trustful of established hierarchies and expects to have a greater voice, especially in the workplace. They have grown up in a socially networked, information-rich environment where transparency and a free flow of ideas are the norm. So, while innovative and highly creative, today's workers often don't see eye to eye with management—they may have opinions of their own about the direction of the organization—and thus relish participation in just about everything they do, whether across social networks or in the office in general. This culture shift is forcing many organizations to rethink their strategies for managing the modern workforce.

An example of this kind of change in action comes from the banking industry, which isn't necessarily known for its cutting-edge management practices. But when Tim Elkins, executive vice president and chief information officer of PrimeLending, a mortgage provider with about 2,500 associates with more than 250 branches across the United States, joined the company six years ago, it took him about six months to acknowledge that something was different about the company's culture. After working in the mortgage lending industry for his entire career, he was used to organizations that relied on traditional top-down hierarchical decision making.

At PrimeLending, Elkins was blown away by how Todd Salmans, the company's CEO, would huddle with his executive team twice a week to share updates from around the company and to solicit ideas, rather than issue top-down directives of his own. "He says things like, 'This is what I'm thinking, what do you think?'" said Elkins. "Ultimately he is the decision maker, but he's actively seeking the input of his direct reports. And that's something that trickles down throughout the organization."[6]

Similarly, Scott Bristol, PrimeLending's president, regularly sends out an e-mail to all employees asking for ideas about how the company could be run better or be a better place. "We've had quite a few wins come through that way," said Elkins. "It proves that people can make a difference at whatever level they work on. Scott responds to every e-mail and it's a great opportunity to get the ear of the president."

As another example of the collaborative nature of PrimeLending's culture, Elkins pointed to the fact that he and his executive vice president peers meet twice a week to talk through not just the good news, but also the challenges each faces on the job. In that way, they work together to solve the company's biggest issues rather than trying to defend their own turf. "One of the mantras we use around here is, 'I've got your back,'" said Elkins. "I've never seen a group of managers at any level that are so open about their struggles because they know we will help each other rather than use it as an opportunity to help themselves."

Elkins said he has applied those same principles to the one-on-one meetings he has with his direct reports, where he allows his team members to set the agenda for what they want to talk about rather than making assumptions about what's most important for them. By rethinking how to interact and collaborate in the workplace, PrimeLending not only has fostered a family-style collaborative culture, but has also produced results: the company has now grown into the fourth-largest purchase mortgage lender for home loans in the United States.

Red Hat's decision-making process also looks fundamentally different from how most conventional organizations approach the process. We have embraced the value of participation, and we expect to involve broad groups of associates in decisions. The best way that I can describe it is that we move most of the change management activities into the decision-making process itself. It often takes longer to reach a decision. The process can be slow and painful. Red Hat leaders sometimes moan when they know they must make a significant change, because they know they're in for a lot of time, debate, and pushback. But the result is that we end up making much better decisions, and perhaps more importantly, we execute on those decisions with speed and efficiency.

Even when Red Hat is dealing with a decision involving confidential information like an acquisition—laws prevent us from sharing that kind of insider information with the investment community—it remains a priority for us to share and communicate what we can with our associates simultaneously or, where possible, even before we reach out to the company's shareholders or the press. In other words, when Red Hat buys another company, we're limited in what we can tell associates and when. But, beyond watching CNBC or reading a press release, Red Hatters also get the news from leadership in a way that stimulates a conversation about why we made the decision and what the company as a whole plans to do next. That means that sometimes you have to make decisions that can be unpopular despite all the work you put in to listen and engage the team. But what you need to do is explain why you think the change is needed. Then, you need to prepare to defend your rationale.

Most conventional organizations aren't well structured to handle this kind of feedback cycle with their employees. It's not enough to simply communicate the results of a decision after the fact. Our solution is to open things up by breaking down conventional organization hierarchies. Specifically, we've embraced the idea of open organization such that the majority of our decisions and management procedures are transparent to our teams. At the same time, we use input and feedback from associates to make decisions. Getting people to engage in the decision-making process doesn't have to be at just the corporate level. It's a mind-set that leaders throughout the organization should wholeheartedly embrace. That's something the creative teams at Pixar practice in what I might call their "open movie-making process." During the making of a movie, everyone involved has the chance to add his or her input to the direction of the project. But, in the end, it's the director who makes the final decisions; like Red Hat, Pixar doesn't operate a democracy where everything is put to a vote. But, as the authors of *Collective Genius* state, "the best directors were those open to a wide diversity of ideas, willing to let people try different approaches, and able to keep possibilities open in their minds."[7]

Consider the story that Lance Phillips, Red Hat's senior director of support for the Americas, told us at an organizational meeting we were attending in Miami in the winter of 2012. Phillips had joined the Red Hat family in 2007 when his prior employer, MetaMatrix, a data integration company based in St. Louis, was acquired so Red Hat could improve its position in the middleware market. Red Hat was interested in improving the way the customer support department operated as well, which is why Phillips was "drafted," as he puts it, into heading up global support for the Americas. "Red Hat liked the fact that all of us at MetaMatrix had a lot of experience," Phillips said. "We were told they were excited to bring in senior managers like me to add value to the organization." In other words, Phillips felt he was expected to bring about serious change.

After commuting from his home in St. Louis to Raleigh for a few months (the original MetaMatrix team remained in St. Louis), Phillips—after long conversations with his wife—eventually settled permanently in North Carolina. Similar to how a consultant might evaluate a new client's challenges, Phillips used his first few months to study and think through the strengths and weaknesses of how the support team was structured. His boss, a vice president, had given him the latitude to drive the change necessary to bolster the support team's effectiveness. When he moved in for good, therefore, he thought he was ready to put his well-thought-out plan in place. "I felt like I had been given the keys to the place and was ready to solve the world's problems," Phillips told me.

Soon thereafter, at one of his leadership team's weekly staff meetings, Phillips unveiled an action plan intended to, as he put it, "turn the ship around and get it pointed in the right direction." The more he talked about his visions for how the support team could be reorganized to best help Red Hat's clients, the more Phillips noticed people shutting down. "Pretty soon I was looking at rows of stone faces," he said.

Unnerved by the experience, Phillips pulled his chief lieutenant, Maria DiMaio, aside to ask her why the meeting had gone so poorly. "We immediately got into a passionate debate where she told me my ideas would never work at Red Hat," Phillips recalled. "I just didn't understand what was happening. I remember going home that night and complaining to my wife that the people at work just didn't understand change management."

For her part, DiMaio, who had been working in the open source software community for years before joining Red Hat, felt that she needed to fight back, because she thought that Phillips was putting the company's culture at risk with his approach to implementing change. "I was going home and telling my husband that I felt like I was arguing myself out of a job," DiMaio said. "But I felt like I had an obligation to represent the tenets of our culture: courage, freedom, and open source. I wasn't telling Lance we couldn't do what he was asking as much as I was telling him we had to go about doing it in a different way."

Of course, it's easy to sympathize with Phillips. After all, he had been hired specifically to bring about change in the support organization. He even had a mandate from a vice president to do what he thought he needed to do. In most organizations, people would simply fall in line and follow their boss's orders. Why, then, wasn't anyone, including DiMaio, his direct report, listening to him and his ideas?

Phillips was particularly frustrated by the fact that the team wasn't buying into his idea of changing where they were seated. Phillips wanted to shift workstations around so that senior team members would sit next to younger and less experienced associates, who served as the first line of defense in answering support calls from customers. That way, when questions and problems came in from customers, the less experienced associates could simply turn around to get help rather than having to send an e-mail or pick up the phone. "I knew that we could share and transfer knowledge very quickly this way," Phillips said.

But senior team members rejected the idea precisely because they didn't want to have to sit next to where the phones rang the most. Facing a stalemate, Phillips quickly realized that he needed to change his entire approach. "If we had simply issued an edict, there would have been a mutiny," he admitted.

To his credit, though, Phillips didn't give up. After realizing that he wasn't going to bring about change simply by issuing orders or by sending out a memo, he brought his team together and struck a bargain: he told them his reasons for why the restructuring made sense and that if they would trust him enough to try it for a while, he would also commit to changing everything back if it wasn't working.

"Lance recognized that solving the problem was not about holding endless discussions or answering every concern before we took action," DiMaio said. "It was more about acknowledging people's concerns and then putting an exit plan in place if things didn't work out. You're always going to have stragglers to deal with, but they're usually a small minority."

As it turned out, everything worked out better than Phillips had dared to hope. Not only is the new structure still in place, but even the most vocal holdouts have admitted to him that working next to the phones "isn't too bad." "I think everyone came to understand that the benefits of the new plan outweighed most of the concerns people had been bringing up," DiMaio said.

The entire experience taught Phillips that in order to bring about change, he had to first explain why change was needed. He also had to listen to everyone's concerns and make alterations to the plan based on that feedback. "Not having power is a scary thing for managers," Phillips admitted. "But if you truly engage individuals by giving that up and embracing an open source process, you actually get real power back because people will follow you because they trust you, not because you ordered them to."

Phillips calls his first encounter with the Red Hat culture the single most frustrating and rewarding experience of his career. "I learned that at Red Hat, almost nothing happens top down," he said. "If you want to change something here, you need to socialize it, pull feedback, and build a movement around that change. The painful part of that process is that, for managers, it takes much longer to get any change effort moving. The benefit, on the other hand, is that the adoption phase of change management is significantly shortened as you theoretically already have the buy-in. This is the key reason, in my opinion, we are so good at change and can keep pace with innovation. It is part of our organizational DNA that we build momentum around change from the bottom up."

Another lesson to learn from Phillips's story is that as a leader, you are the ultimate decision maker. Remember, the company isn't a democracy where everyone has an equal vote. You will sometimes have to make decisions that are decidedly unpopular, despite all the work you put in to listen and engage your team. But, as Phillips demonstrated, what you need to do is explain *why* you think the change is needed. Then, you need to prepare to defend your rationale.

In choosing a software vendor to run our internal operations like payroll, accounting, and accounts payable, I had a similar experience. Because Red Hat is a publicly traded company with global operations and all kinds of reporting complications, few vendors actually make a system that suits our needs. After conducting an in-depth analysis of our needs, we eventually realized that there was only one vendor who could give us what we needed. But there were two major catches: one, the software wasn't open source, and two, the vendor was one of our biggest competitors. It was quite a dilemma.

In most conventional organizations facing similar circumstances, the CEO would simply make the choice and push that decision down through the organization. But that wasn't going to work at Red Hat. The team members making the decision knew that if we didn't take the time to explain it, we would face an internal public relations disaster. So the team went to memo-list to explain why we needed this system and that, unfortunately, there were no open source alternatives to turn to.

The reaction to the post, despite our hopes, was decidedly negative. As the discussion threads grew, people wondered why we just didn't build our own open source product. The reason, I explained, was because of all the complex business rules that go into building such a system and that we didn't have the resources to manage such a system. The equation was simple: we needed the system's capability immediately, and we didn't have time to invest in building our own.

While that eased the grumbling somewhat, it wasn't until a member of the team charged with the decision took to memo-list himself to explain in great detail how he came to make the decision, along with a promise that we would eventually move off our competitor's product as soon as it was feasible. While there are certainly people in the company who will never be satisfied with that decision, the huge positive response that post received—where dozens of people thanked him for explaining his rationale—proved that when you take the time to make your decision-making process transparent, you can still drive progress and get things done, even when your decision is an unpopular one.

There's another lesson for leaders here as well: keep an open mind. While you may be able to push forward unpopular decisions, you should continue to listen to the feedback you're receiving while also constantly evaluating whether your decision was, in the end, the best it could be.

Another example of how open collaboration leads to great decisions involved what we now call the "Billion Dollar Celebration," a coordinated series of events held at Red Hat locations worldwide to mark the year when the company first earned more than $1 billion in annual revenue. The roots of that celebration were planted about a year and half earlier when, at a companywide meeting, I was laying out my vision for how Red Hat would become a billion-dollar company. Someone in the audience then asked how we would celebrate that moment when it arrived. I laughed off the comment and asked DeLisa Alexander, chief people officer, to come up with an answer.

What happened next truly illustrates how things get done at Red Hat. Kim Jokisch, director of the employment branding team that eventually pulled everything together, created a cross-functional team to spearhead the effort. She recruited people from all over the company—including departments like employment branding, corporate events, community affairs, public relations, and facilities management—to work on the project, which would involve time and effort well beyond their day jobs.

"We used design thinking and included different people along the way," says Jokisch, whose team met weekly. Eventually, the team decided to announce the idea for celebration via "The Show," a quarterly internal video program, in which everyone in the company was asked for input. Jokisch also recruited me as part of that effort: picture me in a pointed party hat, asking the audience, with a straight face and a serious voice, to submit their ideas—only to have Jokisch dump a bucket of confetti on my head. The clip ends as I blow a note on a party horn—toot!

Well, either because of—or in spite of—the skit, we got hundreds of responses from Red Hatters all over the world. The team then categorized the ideas and identified several key themes. One common response was that people wanted to give back to the open source communities that had helped Red Hat reach this latest milestone. They also wanted to party and get Red Hat swag of some kind. The fourth key theme was that they wanted us to recognize Red Hat as a truly global company.

To cover all those bases, the team again reached out to members of the Red Hat community for help. First off, we asked Melanie Chernoff, who heads up Red Hat's charitable contribution efforts, to put together a short list of four organizations that Red Hat might want to acknowledge. We then took the list that Chernoff and the community relations committee identified and asked everyone in the company to vote on a favorite. Each organization would then receive a percentage of the money budgeted for the pot based on how many responses it received (that is, if an organization got 30 percent of the votes, it would receive 30 percent of the money). Everyone in the company had a sense of ownership in the process and a chance to vote for the organization they were most passionate about.

The committee also turned to the community for help in planning the party—or, more accurately—the dozens of parties that were going to be held simultaneously worldwide. The team worked with the finance department and office managers around the globe to set budgets and then let every office decide how it wanted to celebrate in its own unique way. In Australia, Red Hatters went swimming with dolphins. In England, they took country-western line-dancing lessons. In Raleigh, we rented out a convention center and held a carnival that included inflatable bounce houses and laser tag. Jokisch's team, along with several executives, fanned out and captured many of the celebrations on video, which were subsequently shared via

"The Show" so everyone could connect and see how their fellow Red Hatters liked to celebrate.

When it came to the swag, every Red Hat associate received a branded champagne flute that we all used to hoist a beverage of choice as I made my toast, which was webcast around the world to every Red Hat office. The event was a massive success that is talked about reverently, even today.

As Jokisch told me, "We didn't go into this in any prescribed way. We let the best ideas win and worked collaboratively and transparently to bring it all together. It's really a great example of how we get things done the Red Hat way."

Leader's Role: Making Transparent Decisions

Here's another example that illustrates how Red Hatters collect feedback as they work through their decision-making processes. Not long after I became CEO, I realized that the organization's vision statement did not provide a direct link to our associates' day-to-day actions:

> *To be the defining technology company of the 21st century, and through our actions strengthen the social fabric by continually democratizing content and technology.*

While this statement showed the scale of our ambition—to be the defining technology company of the twenty-first century—I got the distinct impression that many people didn't understand what it meant or what it was telling them to do. As the company was entering new markets and experiencing tremendous growth, we clearly needed to refocus and refine our mission to serve as a unifying direction.

In most conventional organizations, like Delta Air Lines, the solution would have been easy: I, as CEO, would convene a small group of senior executives who, along with the help of an eloquent consultant, would craft the company's mission statement during a weekend retreat. Once complete, it would simply be distributed to the rest of the company. Shazam! Job done.

What really happens in these cases is that, no matter how many copies of the mission statement you print out and hang by the coffee pot or near the soda machine, the result is always the same: nobody remembers it. One executive I knew, when he visited other companies, carried a $50 bill with him to use as a challenge. He would give that $50 to anyone who could recite the company's mission statement. Guess what? He still has his $50.

Luckily for me, my team knew the conventional top-down approach wouldn't work at Red Hat. Our mission needed to emerge from within. For the mission to truly resonate with associates, they needed to be the ones to create it. So we decided to do our best to ensure that everyone in the company would have a chance to participate.

Even as I began discussing the mission statement, a passionate group of folks had already come together and had begun thinking about how to solve the problem. These people had joined forces to ensure that Red Hat's corporate mission wasn't just words on paper, but instead was deeply embedded within the organization. They had quickly come to the conclusion Red Hat needed something more directional than the phrase "defining technology company" to connect the overall vision to the strategic plan.

By the time they approached me, the team had already crafted some sample mission statements for me to look at. We gathered around and looked at all of the things they had come up with, debating the merits of each. In a few short hours of work, we developed a statement that felt pretty comfortable to all of us. But then we did something most companies wouldn't dream of doing. Rather than going straight to the senior executives to get their opinions first or continuing to muck around with the words for weeks or months to get them just perfect, we employed an open source technique our engineers sometimes refer to as "release early, release often."

Instead of crafting the company mission behind closed doors, we showed it to the whole company via memo-list and my blog. In draft form. Before it was perfect. And we asked everyone what they thought of it. We asked which parts resonated most. We asked them what we should change. We asked for suggestions to make it better. Anyone could give feedback, and many did. There was thoughtful discussion, some fantastic suggestions for changing wording, even some argument and disagreement about whether this truly reflected what the company was trying to achieve. This was a conversation the company needed to have.

One key benefit of this approach was that it engaged many thoughtful associates in a discussion about why they were doing their jobs. Rarely during a hectic day (especially in a growing technology company) do people take the time to think about the forest and not just the trees. Opening up the process of defining the Red Hat mission gave them an excuse to do exactly that. But perhaps the biggest benefit was that, by asking associates to become a part of the process, and then taking some of their best feedback and using it to improve the mission itself, we gave them ownership of the mission.

In the open source world, we believe the best ideas should win, no matter where they come from. Yet in many organizations, it is not possible for the best ideas to win, because they are hidden in the brains of people who sit many layers deep in the organization. The best ideas get lost as they make their way up through the hierarchy. We cut through the hierarchy and took our draft of the mission statement right to the people to whom it mattered most. We were able to get the best ideas, unfiltered by management, and apply them right away.

Using a fully transparent process to create our mission statement was a huge success. It resonates with our people because it is a statement about not only *what* we do, but also *how* we do it. But you can judge for yourself:

> *To be the catalyst in communities of customers, contributors, and partners creating better technology the open source way.*

Allowing ideas to come from anywhere, opening up the creation of the mission so that anyone could contribute early in the process, promoting discussion and dialogue, and then finally allowing the best ideas to win—this is how we created our mission the open source way. The result is a great example of how our associates drove a much better answer than a few executives (no matter how talented) could have done on their own. Associates were engaged and pleased with the output. In the end, not only did we create a meaningful mission statement, I would also wager that most, if not all, Red Hatters could cite it by heart.

Slower Decisions Lead to Faster Results

Why would anyone go through all this work? It clearly slows decision making down. It sucks up massive amounts of time for everyone. It's frustrating. At times, it's even infuriating. As a leader, it challenges your ego; having people question, question, and question every decision you make is not fun. So why do it? The simple answer is because it leads to better decisions, better engagement, better execution, and ultimately better results.

Making decisions is easy compared to actually putting the ideas involved in the decision into action, especially when your goal is to change something. The rub, though, according to a 2004 study called "Boosting Business Performance through Programme and Project Management" by PricewaterhouseCoopers (PwC), is that a majority of companies, 59 percent, realize a negative ROI when they undergo a major business improvement program.[8] That means that companies don't get much (if anything) for the money they invest in big decisions.

The PwC study found that the three biggest reasons projects failed to achieve their desired payoffs were due to:

- A lack of commitment and follow-through by senior executives.

- Defective project management skills among middle managers.

- Lack of training of and confusion among frontline employees.

The companies that achieved the best results, on the other hand, could boast that:

- Senior and middle managers and frontline employees were all involved.

- Everyone's responsibilities were clear.

- Reasons for the project were understood and accepted throughout the organization.

This study highlights some of the big reasons why the field of change management has blossomed throughout the corporate world in recent years, where companies like my former employer, BCG, help shepherd such projects. For instance, to save money, a large publishing company might decide to change how it prints and distributes its books. To help ensure that the changes needed in people and technology go smoothly, it hires a firm like BCG to help drive participation and engagement throughout the organization to bring about the desired changes.

At Red Hat, we do things differently. We strive for change management to happen during the decision process, not during execution. We've learned that to bring about changes, it's not enough to simply sell our associates on a decision after it has been made. Rather, as in the example of our mission statement, associates feel more ownership in the changes needed when they are involved in making the decision behind them.

Consider the power of the practice that the manufacturer SRC Holdings calls "high-involvement planning," a semiannual process in which department heads lay out their vision for where their part of the organization is headed in both short and long terms—as far as five to ten years out. In combination, they then explain the strategies and contingency plans that will help them move closer to their goal. Anyone in the organization can then respond to those strategies—asking questions or offering suggestions—before weighing in with how confident they are in the plan. In other words, before a plan is put into action, leaders get the opportunity to create buy-in among their associates about where they are headed together. Since everyone has a chance to weigh in on the plans, it greatly reduces the finger-pointing and blaming that is so common, especially when unexpected hurdles pop up. "We have strength in numbers in contributing toward the direction of the organization," said CEO Jack

Stack. "With our different viewpoints, we can come up with the best solutions and course of action."[9]

Other recent examples at Red Hat in which we have employed a similar inclusive approach to major companywide decisions include the development of the overall strategy and branding plans, both projects that are led by my longtime colleague Jackie Yeaney, who now heads up strategy and marketing at Red Hat and also worked with me at BCG and Delta. In most companies, senior leaders and consultants forge corporate strategy and marketing plans—like mission statements—and then unveil them to the rest of the company. Just as often, those strategy documents usually end up gathering dust on a bookshelf, unused and ignored despite the money and time that went into creating them.

That's not the case at Red Hat. In 2008, we embarked on our first formal strategic planning process. I was new to the company and felt we needed to more formally articulate our medium-term goals (three to five years) and the key initiatives required across the company to get there. That's when I asked Yeaney to help. Traditionally, this process is very top down. A small strategic planning group works with senior leaders to develop the plan. But, as you know by now, that would never fly at Red Hat. Yeaney immediately set to work involving the company in building a road map for where our strategy was headed. By engaging an initial roster of leaders who would then connect with their teams, she put in motion a series of concentric circles like ripples on a lake that eventually touched everyone. But instead of ripples that moved only outward from her, they continued back and forth as they carried information and ideas throughout the company. The result was that rather than senior leaders like Yeaney and me brainstorming where we thought the company should head, we got feedback from the people closest to the frontline action with the latest information that could help drive the process effectively.

As Yeaney wrote in a paper about the entire process titled, "Democratizing the Corporate Strategy Process at Red Hat," "Red Hat is truly a meritocracy of ideas—where the best ideas can come from anywhere in the organization. Many of Red Hat's most successful products and services were built upon the hard work, passion, and commitment of one or more brilliant people inside (or even outside) the organization, not a top-down mandate. With this all in mind we knew we would have to make sure our process was democratized; less top-down, more all-around."

There is a saying at BCG that discovered logic is more powerful than delivered logic. In the BCG context, this described why we liked having our clients involved in projects. When clients helped reach the conclusions about where they were headed (in building a strategy document, acquiring a new business, or simply plotting their future course), they were much more likely to buy into it. And guess what? The likelihood of our recommendations being successfully implemented rose dramatically. The same principles apply to making decisions in your own company and involving your own people. The more transparent you make the decision-making process, the more effectively you can turn those decisions into real action that everyone can engage in.

Yeaney said in her paper: "From the beginning, we put engaging with our associates ahead of communicating to them. The entire company needed to own the strategy if we wanted to see it implemented. Associates needed to be an integral part of developing and implementing it." Building engagement with all your associates is a challenge that gets bigger relative to the size of your payroll. You're likely going to have to invest more time and effort than you would by simply delegating to a small team of consultants. But as the PwC study reminds us, you're not going to get the kind of results you're looking for. At Red Hat, for example, it took Yeaney five months just to gather information from our associates.

The result, however, has been that Yeaney and I have never seen an organization follow through on its plan over a four-year period as Red Hat has. Yes, it took a sizable commitment of resources to get everyone to buy into the plan. But, by doing so, we've experienced tremendous success. As Yeaney summarized it: "Since we started this process in 2008, Red Hat has been executing more efficiently on its best opportunities, and it shows. Red Hat has grown from $400 million in revenue to more than $1.5 billion and the stock price has quadrupled."

Deciding Inside Out

We've been able to apply these same principles and processes of decision making in involving not just Red Hatters, but our customers and partners as well. That's something other organizations have also begun to embrace. For example, every five years Whole Foods brings together representatives of its primary stakeholder groups to collaborate in designing the next five-year strategic vision through a process it calls "Future Search," in which customers and vendors participate alongside other company stakeholder groups to shape plans for Whole Foods' future.[10]

At Red Hat, we do something along these lines that we call the Red Hat Summit. It's a nearly weeklong event where we bring customers, partners, community enthusiasts, and Red Hatters—from across the globe—together in person. In 2014, for example, we held the summit in San Francisco and attracted thousands of attendees who participated in a series of nearly two hundred different sessions, panel discussions, hands-on labs, and more.

The summit has become a way for associates to connect in deep and meaningful ways with customers, which makes it an incredibly vital part of Red Hat's future success. "The summit allows us to create more opportunities to have face-to-face conversations with our customers and community enthusiasts about what's important to them and how we can help," said Leigh Blaylock, who, as Red Hat's manager of content marketing, plays an integral role in successfully orchestrating the coordination of the summit content.

Most companies hold similar customer-focused events, but what makes the Red Hat Summit unique is how we go about setting the agenda. In most companies, the speakers, classes, and breakout sessions for their events are established in an efficient, top-down manner. But at Red Hat, we do it differently and we have for a long time.

In the open source world, many conferences are organized in a free-form and informal manner, where the participants themselves set the agenda. An example is BarCamp, an international network of user-generated "unconferences" where, at the start of the conference, people who want to make a presentation tape the name of the session they propose on a board along with all other suggestions. Once complete, participants then vote on which sessions they want to attend, which results in the agenda for the conference.

While that kind of decentralized planning works well with small groups, we can't employ the exact same method for planning the summit for thousands of people. But we also don't want to lose what makes the BarCamp approach so special by implementing a conventional top-down process. Instead we start out with a ten-person screening committee from different departments that taps our internal communities and works from the bottom up to identify the different tracks to cover at the event, like IT efficiency or business and strategy alignment. We then issue a request for proposals from all communities—including customers and partners—for specific session, panel, and lab ideas. In 2014, we received a total of 686 proposals. Obviously, that's a lot to choose from.

But, again, rather than make the pruning decision top down or marketing driven, we create a cross-functional selection subcommittee composed of nearly 150 Red Hatters who represent several departments and all regions, to make the agenda decisions. Subcommittee members are nominated by an eighteen-person main selection committee, which includes representatives who know IT needs best, like our own IT team, and those who know customers best, like engineering, support, and sales. Members from both committees tend to be Red Hatters who have strong reputations within the company.

Subcommittee members rate and comment on sessions via an online tool, which the main selection committee uses to discuss and debate the various proposals via Etherpad, an open source document collaboration tool that records everyone's contributions in real time. "Each person's contributions are tracked with a different color, and those documents get pretty colorful, as you can imagine," said Blaylock. Members of the committee also rely on past speaker ratings and session feedback notes, which have been kept since the 2009 summit, as a way to ensure that the best ideas win—and the best speakers return—as objectively as possible. Once the debate concludes, the agenda has been set.

The key point, clearly, is that by applying the notion of a meritocracy to the process of choosing summit sessions, we wind up with a compelling and wide-ranging agenda that delivers incredible value and learning to all those who attend, particularly because customers and partners are active participants in the entire event. Partners and customers frequently say that the Red Hat Summit has more authenticity and passion than a typical IT conference. I firmly believe that the difference is in our decision-making process.

Getting Started

The good news about inclusive decision making is that it's easy to start. You can simply ask a few others (or two or ten) for their thoughts on a decision you are making. Unlike engagement, which I argue in chapter 3 is an all-or-nothing proposition, inclusive decision making is a continuum. As a leader, you can experiment with how broadly to include others.

The bad news is that you will find that many people do not want to participate. Not everyone wants to be a leader or make decisions that affect others. It also takes time for groups to rewire themselves to make decisions. Including broader parts of your organization in decision making is something to approach incrementally.

Jim's Leadership Tips

1. *When you make your next decision, reflect on whether it was influenced by others' points of view.* If so, did their influence change your decision? If not, how might the decision have been different if you had considered others' perspectives?

2. *Ask one or two thought leaders on your team their opinions on something you're considering.* They won't question your competence or decisiveness. They'll feel flattered.

3. *Before making your next decision, ask yourself whether others will be surprised.* If so, think about including them before finalizing it.

4. *Pick an issue and try openly discussing it with a broader group, whether in a staff meeting or an informal gathering.* After a while, it will become natural.

5. *Try to observe the difference in execution of decisions that were made openly, with input, versus those that truly came from the top down.*

7

Catalyzing Direction

The purpose of the new management model called the open organization is to build an organization capable of thriving in the new economy—an organization that can respond quickly to external changes without relying on running things up the chain of command. An open organization encourages and fosters initiative and creativity among its members rather than, as Andrew McAfee of the MIT Center for Digital Business puts it, running operations based on "HiPPO—the highest-paid person's opinion."[1] The new model that is evolving also appeals to a new generation of employees whose expectations are vastly different from those of people who preceded them in the workplace.

A core function of management systems that I've yet to discuss is setting direction. Traditionally, direction is set at the top. The typical structural solution at most companies includes a strategy or strategic planning department. These organizations typically have a handful of bright MBAs with skills and training in strategic frameworks, planning, and the like. Working with senior management and perhaps a few consultants, they help craft the core strategies that the organization ultimately follows. Strategic directives are then handed down for execution throughout the company. It's simply assumed at most companies that the senior executive team and the board of directors set strategy.

Obviously, top-down directives don't do well in open organizations. So, given this new type of organization, if you have all these engaged and passionate people ready to take on the world, how do you, as a leader, set the *direction* in which the company is going? If you can't just issue an order and say, "We're going to take that hill!" then how do you get the organization to do different things, or do things differently? How do you as a leader get everyone in a participative company to change or to move together in the same direction?

Introducing the Catalyst in Chief

After my first year at Red Hat, I began to wonder what my role as the president and CEO truly was. By that point I'd begun to understand and appreciate both the power and the subtlety of Red Hat's culture and participative management model. Clearly, continuing to drive and reinforce the system was job one. But what was less clear to me was the role I needed to play in driving changes in strategic direction. I'm sure many other Red Hat leaders have asked themselves that same question.

The answer came to me as I reflected on our mission statement. As you might remember from chapter 6, it reads: "To be the catalyst in communities of customers, contributors, and partners creating better technology the open source way." The more I thought about this, the more I realized that the answer was right in front of me. My role as a leader was to be the catalyst for the organization itself.

One of the most difficult and subtle parts of fine-tuning that statement was settling on the right word (or words) to describe the role Red Hat aspires to play in the open source communities in which we operate. In early drafts, we used the word "leader." But many people involved in the process quickly pointed out that this word wasn't entirely accurate. Leadership, in their view, implies a level of control that we at Red Hat do not have, nor aspire to have, within our communities. We treasure the concept of meritocracy, and calling Red Hat the leader seemed to imply that somehow the rules didn't apply to us.

We next tried substituting the phrase "active participant." That was softer and more accurately described how we contribute to the communities in which we're involved, but again, it wasn't quite right. We aspire to do more than just contribute; we want to influence the direction of these communities, yet not control them either.

Ultimately, we arrived at the word "catalyst"—"an agent that provokes or speeds significant change or action"—and I think it best describes how Red Hat provides leadership in the communities in which we operate. We contribute to our communities, doing what we believe is in their best long-term interest, by building up positions of thought leadership within. In that way, Red Hat serves as an agent that provokes or speeds change or action in the open source communities in which we operate. The more I thought about it, the more I realized that this concept also provides a good model for the role of leaders in the twenty-first century.

Leaders have many opportunities to act as an "agent." We have the ability to call meetings and talk about what we think is important, to ask questions and get answers, and to structure areas of work. All are opportunities to catalyze direction. I'm not a chemist, so a good mental image for me is to think about a dock piling at an ocean shore. Look at any piling and you'll see an abundance of sea life attached to it. Barnacles attach to the piling and then attract additional sea life, which feeds on the barnacles and might also make a home there. Before you know it, there's an entire mini-ecosystem around that piling. But if the piling were not there, none of that sea life would have chosen to grow at that exact spot. The piling created the context and vehicle for life to congregate. Simply by being there, it fosters a new community, which is a key dynamic of catalyzing an open organization.

But there are also moves—some subtle, others more overt—that you can take to sway the kind of actions that your participative community undertakes.

The Leader's Role: Leverage Your Soap Box

One of the benefits of being a leader is that you have the power to create venues for bringing people together, and you have the power to set the agenda for a range of conversations throughout the organization. After being at Red Hat for several years, I hope that I have personally earned the right to be heard in our meritocracy. But even in our culture, my title certainly helps. Generally, because of my role, people will make the time to listen to me, and they will seriously consider what I've said. I get their attention. When and how I, as a leader, use those venues can be a powerful way for me to influence the direction of the company.

When I address the company either in a formal way, say, at a quarterly company meeting, or in more informal settings, like the ad hoc town hall–style Q&As I hold in our global offices, what I talk about, the questions I ask, and the issues I raise foster discussion and debate throughout the entire company. I have the opportunity to light little sparks and see what passionate fires erupt from there. But because I am only offering a spark, it's the subsequent conversations people have with their peers throughout the organization that truly result in things happening.

I am not talking about announcing formal initiatives that have already been fully vetted and decided upon. That's nothing more than personally delivering a top-down decision. Rather, I use these opportunities to poke and prod on issues that I believe are important to Red Hat. The subsequent conversations and activities around the company will ultimately coalesce into the appropriate initiatives. My job as catalyst is to stir the debate and ignite the conversations. From there, our associates, through their own conversations and debate, will drive the ultimate actions.

For instance, Red Hat has emerged as a leader in the field of cloud computing. We are the leading contributors to and sellers of the infrastructure software used to run public and private clouds. The specific initiatives to establish that position didn't emerge from a top-down strategy process. They came from the senior team at Red Hat describing how important it was for Red Hat and open source to emerge as the default choice for next-generation IT infrastructure. That's as directive as we needed to be. Myriad debates have subsequently raged within the company over specific technologies, markets, and business models. Those debates have and are leading to much better execution than we could ever have prescribed from the top down. Frankly, the market changes so rapidly that any structured plan would be obsolete in months. Instead, the people closer to the facts and activities in the marketplace are making the decisions on the specifics. And they are empowered to react quickly, which keeps our strategies from getting stale.

Whole Foods operates in a similar way. Since the company continues to expand rapidly, it now has four hundred stores but has a goal of eventually operating twelve hundred.[2] It couldn't possibly hope to keep up with all the trends and tastes of those local markets through a centralized command system. Rather, CEO John Mackey has made it clear that regions and stores have the freedom to experiment with a mix of non–Whole Foods–branded products as they see fit. That's especially true when it comes to how those stores support the burgeoning local foods movement, says Mackey, "which allows a constant supply of new and innovative products to bubble up from local sources, with the most successful ones eventually spreading across the company."[3] To put that another way, Mackey allows his leaders at the regional and store levels to essentially chart the future mix of products for the entire company as a whole because he trusts that they know and care about the company's purpose and mission. That's powerful stuff.

Obviously, leveraging a soapbox requires that venues exist where leaders are interacting with their employees. Having a regular cadence of opportunities for these types of interactions is critical. At Red Hat, we have quarterly company meetings, though because of our size and global spread, most associates dial in by phone or via their computer to access them. We do, however, have vehicles for associates to e-mail questions or ask during conference calls. I still find face-to-face interactions are most productive. Time zones and distance can be barriers, so the senior team and I try to schedule town hall meetings when we visit locations worldwide. Within Red Hat, I'm not alone. Many Red Hat managers and leaders create similar forums within their own organizations. Every company is different, but regardless, ensuring that venues for interaction exist should be a priority.

Selling Half-Baked Thoughts

Often leaders have a general sense of where they want to lead the company, but have not yet nailed down the specifics. Unfortunately, too often leaders are uncomfortable sharing plans that aren't complete. They worry that they are not setting clear goals or that ambiguity will cause more harm than good. In a participative organization, this is a great time to engage. It often means articulating aspirational goals (as long as they are consistent with the purpose and values) without specifics on how to get there. Particularly when the specific implementation steps aren't yet clear, involving associates early is a great way to help identify priorities and create alignment throughout the organization. The goal, in short, is to make the most of the knowledge and skills of the broader organization to fill in the details. As Daniel Goleman, author of the influential book *Emotional Intelligence*, describes in his definition of "primal leadership," there is an emotional dimension to leadership where a leader's primary task is to "articulate a message that resonates with their followers' emotional reality, with their sense of purpose—and so to move people in a positive direction. Leadership, after all, is the art of getting work done through other people."[4]

For example, as I've described throughout the book, Red Hat has built an extremely successful business by catalyzing open source communities. It's deep in our DNA and is our source of competitive advantage. It allows the company to deliver cutting-edge technology at dramatically lower prices than our competitors can provide. In short, our competitive advantage is built around a capability to leverage open source. Since we do deliver such a great value proposition, customers generally like us. Surveys suggest that we have very high levels of customer satisfaction, and we receive very high Net Promoter scores—a high percentage of our customers say they will recommend Red Hat to friends or other potential customers.

However, as Red Hat has grown and the customer base has expanded beyond the early adopters who are technology savvy and value the technical merits of our solutions, I've worried about whether the company is truly focused on the needs of our mainstream customers. While organizations like the New York Stock Exchange Euronext and DreamWorks care about the performance of our products, most mainstream IT customers care more about issues like ease of use and quality of documentation. In addition, as Red Hat has become a larger part of our customers' IT infrastructure, and as they begin to use more of our products, they expect us to understand their businesses. They expect us to offer solutions to their problems, not just offer great technology.

So clearly Red Hat needs to become more customer focused as it grows. The question is where to start. Some areas are clearly apparent, like making products easier to install. No one would disagree with that. Other areas are subtler. For instance, we need to ensure that our product road maps meet the needs of customers, such as by including ease-of-use features. But that's not necessarily what open source focuses on. Open source is known for driving great technical solutions, and developers pride themselves on offering tremendous flexibility to the user. But they frankly don't worry as much about whether the resulting products are simple to use. It's almost a badge of honor to "drop to the command line," which is techno-speak for using a text-based, terminal window that looks like it's from circa 1970. So while I clearly want Red Hat to listen to customer needs and be responsive, I also recognize our core source of competitive advantage is built on using the power of open source.

In a conventional organization, the answer to my desire to improve customer focus would be to form a team to develop recommendations on a plan. The team would analyze products and processes and would develop a set of recommendations for where to improve customer focus. The team would also look at areas of potential conflict, like customers' desire for ease of use. It would recommend specific initiatives and actions. I would then announce a "focus on the customer" initiative that would be rolled out across the company.

At Red Hat, I can effect the same result by simply talking about it. Using my stage, I "sold" the idea that this is an important thing for us all to address. I explained how, by listening to and working more closely with our customers, we might make the technology even more powerful and the company more successful as a whole. I also explained my concerns about the trade-offs of staying on the bleeding edge of technology and also being responsive to mainstream customers. But that was it. I didn't lay out any specifics about how we could go about making ourselves more customer focused. I didn't charter a team. Rather, I laid out the context that helped illustrate how critical moving in that direction could be for the future of the company. In that way, what I was selling was a "half-baked" idea.

What happened was that people throughout the organization began to do things to improve engagement with customers. Multiple initiatives emerged across the company. For instance, Marco Bill-Peter, who heads Red Hat's global support organization, took up the challenge in his own way. Without any direct orders issued from me, he created a unique approach to solving customers' problems. Rather than the conventional approach in which a customer calling with a complex problem would be bounced around before he or she would finally connect with the expert who could actually solve the issue, Bill-Peter and his team came up with the concept of a "swarm," which comprised cross-departmental teams of service reps and engineers with different levels of knowledge capable of handling just about any kind of issue. That meant that any time a customer called in, he or she was connected with a team that was motivated to find a solution rather than just punting the ball farther down the line.

Just as importantly, the introduction of the swarm doubled the number of customers who engaged with us, while simultaneously cutting the cost of support as a percentage of the company's overall revenue. The results earned Bill-Peter and his team accolades from around the industry and from publications like *The Economist*, which wrote a case study about Red Hat's innovative solution to delivering enhanced customer service. The swarm approach to connecting and engaging with customers has become so effective that teams across the business—from product documentation to legal—are starting to form and join swarms. "As a company, we see this collaborative model going into other fields," Bill-Peter told *The Economist*. "It leads to innovation across the business and makes people think about how they do things."[5]

More to my point in this chapter, Bill-Peter heard me and went about connecting the dots in his own way to tie Red Hat more closely to customers, which is something he admits he would not have had the freedom to do at his former employer, the tech giant Hewlett-Packard. That's a great thing, because I'm not sure I would have been able to think of doing such a thing myself and then trying to get someone else to implement it. Again, Bill-Peter wasn't following an order; he made up his own mind that it was an important task to undertake, and he and his team came up with their own unique way to implement a solution.

I am convinced that the resulting activities that we've undertaken are better than we would have identified with a formal team. I'm comfortable admitting that I just don't have all the answers, and that no ad hoc team can fully specify all the appropriate activities. By having capable, engaged people recognize the importance of the goal and then expecting them to solve it in their own way, thousands of small tweaks can be made across the company. That's much richer and subtler than the handful of big initiatives that a top-down planning process would generate. And things happen much, much faster throughout the organization than if I wanted to control every decision that was made on a regular basis.

Establishing the Right Amount of Structure

Part of the art of leading a self-directing, engaged organization is to spark the organization to action. The specificity of those goals and targets can vary along a spectrum from ultra-specific numeric targets against discrete objectives to very macro-level, subjective notions like "We need to improve." If your aim is too precise, you might turn people off or send them in the wrong direction by giving them too much direction. At the same time, if you make the goals too broad, you might not inspire any action whatsoever or be left with utter chaos as people run off in multiple directions at the same time. So the goal is to try and create enough structure around the organization's actions without creating too much. Finding the balance is a real art.

W. L. Gore is noted for its complete lack of hierarchy, despite having nine thousand associates spread among thirty countries. The company intentionally keeps its teams small, two hundred people or fewer, as a way to foster creativity and innovation. Gary Hamel has written extensively about the company and about its founder Bill Gore, who wanted his company to have a "lattice" as its base for a corporate structure where there were "no layers of management, information would flow freely in all directions, and personal communications would be the norm. And individuals and self-managed teams would go directly to anyone in the organization to get what they needed to be successful."[6] In a conversation with Hamel, Terri

Kelly, Gore's CEO, talked about how its teams, not the leaders at the top, make the decisions that drive the company forward because they are trusted to act in the best interests of the company:

> *First of all, there are norms of behavior and guidelines we follow . . . Every associate understands how important these values are, so when leaders make decisions, people want to understand the "why." They know they have the right to challenge, they have the right to know why this decision is the right one for the company . . . [O]ur leaders have to do an incredible job of internal selling to get the organization to move. The process is sometimes frustrating, but we believe that if you spend more time up front, you'll have associates who are not only fully bought-in, but committed to achieving the outcome. Along the way, they'll also help to refine the idea and make the decision better.[7]*

In the example I shared about Red Hat's increased customer focus, we as a management team were intentionally broad when introducing the concept. Everyone should have a sense for how his or her role ultimately translates to customer value, so it should resonate with everyone. In addition, I had no specific areas that I wanted to ensure were addressed. So we simply stated the problem and asked the organization to respond. There are other times when adding a bit of structure can be helpful. Take, for example, efforts to increase the share of users who opt to pay for Red Hat Enterprise Linux, versus choosing another paid or free Linux distribution. This was a key opportunity that we identified in our strategic planning process. We believe that we add tremendous value in our paid-for subscription version. Since Linux is free, however, there are obviously many alternatives in the marketplace for which users don't have to buy a subscription.

From research, we knew that there were three major areas of opportunity: people using our product but without an active subscription, people who had used to subscribe but let their subscriptions lapse, and people using free, community versions of Linux. Maybe the organization could address all three areas from a simple high-level challenge to address "free to paid," but I worried that some areas might not realize their importance in solving the problem. Without a doubt, engineering and sales would jump in and begin working to better communicate our value proposition and improve usability, but my team and I realized that much of the work required to address unpaid usage of the product and renewals would come from other areas of the business. So the team worried that, without a bit more direction, a broad statement of "free to paid" would send some groups scurrying, while others would feel it was not relevant to their area.

Renewals are a great example. Obviously, for a subscription business, renewals are a key value driver. Much of what drives renewals is hard-core operational work. Because our products are often sold preloaded on a manufacturer's hardware or sold in less developed areas through multiple distribution levels, we often do not know who the end customer is. Improving renewals entails working on myriad operational and legal issues. It involves substantial IT work to improve internal data. We have to work with partners to encourage and motivate them to drive renewals and write tighter contracts with distribution partners to share end-user information where appropriate. Without providing a specific initiative—around which to catalyze this work—many of our operations associates would not have recognized the vital role that they play every day in ensuring customers continue to enjoy the benefits of Red Hat subscriptions.

A similar dynamic of people and activities exists in addressing customers who were using subscriptions without paying for them. So the solution we came up with—to ensure that we addressed all the major areas of "free to fee"—was to break the larger issue down into three more manageable ones:

> *Subscription education:* Developing programs to identify and educate organizations that are using subscriptions but not paying us for them.
>
> *Renewals:* Focusing on many operational, technical, and process issues to ensure that we know what subscriptions are about to expire and that someone at Red Hat or a partner is asking that customer to renew.
>
> *Community-to-enterprise:* Improving products and better communicating the value of a relationship with Red Hat relative to other alternatives.

Once we identified these groups, internal teams tackled the specifics of how to solve them, and they did an amazing job. The results have been fantastic. Again, the goal was to find that sweet spot at which we could create enough structure so that people knew where we wanted to make progress, while also having the freedom to come up with their own ideas for meeting their goals.

Avoiding the Big Mistakes

Many people who read about this distributed—and let's face it, chaotic—approach to driving strategy might think that it sounds like a recipe for disaster. Obviously, all of the various initiatives that emerge haven't been fully analyzed and vetted in the way that top-down initiatives typically are. Isn't that risky? Won't many fail? The simple answer is yes. Some of the things we try fail, though I'm not sure the failure rate is higher than with top-down initiatives. I feel pretty certain that it's lower. Still, without proper top-down vetting, how do we know if we are taking undue levels of risk? How do we identify efforts that aren't working before we squander large amounts of resources on them?

Open source development communities solve this problem by focusing on making many small, incremental changes rather than a few large ones in what's typically referred to as "release early, release often." A key issue in any software project is the risk of errors, or bugs, in the code. Obviously, the more changes are lumped together in one release of software, the greater the likelihood that the release will also introduce bugs. So open source developers have found that by releasing early and often, they can reduce the risk that any release has major problems. Over time, we've observed that this methodology not only reduces the risk of bugs, but also leads to greater innovation. It turns out that making many small improvements continuously ultimately creates more innovation. Perhaps this shouldn't be surprising. One key tenet of modern manufacturing process methodologies, like *kaizen* or lean, is to continually focus on small, iterative improvements.

As Clay Shirky, author of *Here Comes Everybody*, comments about open source: "Because anyone can try anything, the projects that fail, fail quickly, but the people working on those projects can migrate just as quickly to the things that are visibly working. Unlike the business landscape, where companies have an incentive to hide both successes (for reasons of competitive advantage) and failures (to forestall any perception of weakness), open source projects advertise their successes and get failure for free."[8]

Like so many other aspects of its management system, Red Hat has adopted this same principle for internal initiatives. We call our internal corollary to release early, release often "failing fast." Failing fast recognizes that many things we try may not work. But rather than spending tons of time trying to analyze which will work and which will not, we allow many small experiments. Those that gain momentum continue to grow, while those that don't are allowed to wither away. In this way, we can try many things without any single one creating too much risk for the company.

This is a powerful way to allocate resources. For example, people often ask me how we decide which open source projects to commercialize. Though we sometimes initiate projects, most often we simply become involved in existing ones. A small group of engineers—sometimes a single person—begins contributing as an open source community. If the community begins to thrive and our customers begin to get involved, we increase our effort. If not, the engineers move to a new project. By the time we decide to commercialize an offering, the project has grown to the point where the decision is obvious. Projects of all kinds, beyond just software, naturally emerge throughout Red Hat until it's obvious to everyone that someone needs to work on it full-time.

The concept of making small, incremental advances and failing fast aren't unique to open source and Red Hat. Scott Cook, founder of software company Intuit, which makes Quicken and TurboTax, among other products, once said, "When the bosses make the decisions, decisions are made by politics, persuasion, and PowerPoint. When you make decisions through experiment, the best idea can prove itself." I was so taken with that notion that I searched and found more about his philosophy. "I believe the new skill in leadership is leadership by experiment," Cook once told an audience. "In other words, decisions made by having a hypothesis that you then test."[9]

That concept is also related to what electronics giant National Instruments (NI) calls "ooch by ooch." "To "ooch" things means to sort of inch them along, taking small, incremental steps, while avoiding unnecessary risks," NI CEO James Truchard has commented. "You don't need a home run, just persistence."[10]

Unanswered Questions Remain

While Red Hat's leadership and management system evolved organically out of the open source software movement, it remains a work in progress. We continue to seek ways to tweak and improve it to meet the demands of running, in our case, a twenty-first-century public company. An area of particular interest for me is how to be the best leader possible in this new environment. As we have begun to think of leaders more as catalysts than dictators or generals, I've learned firsthand how leaders—including CEOs—need to adapt to the new dynamics involved in leading participative communities if they want to reap the benefits of speed and innovation from them.

For example, in my role as catalyst, I strive to encourage debate and discussion about the direction in which we want to move as an organization. But a key question then becomes, "How long do you let debates rage?" Or even, "How decisive should a leader be?" Those questions are tough to answer, especially at Red Hat where debates can last literally for months on end, maybe even years if they involve anything related to open source versus proprietary software.

But while it might seem clear that a debate that goes on for too long becomes unproductive and a drain on time and resources, it's a constant struggle not to step in too soon and create serious engagement issues as a result. The truth is that I'm not sure there is a right or wrong answer to the question of how long you allow debates to continue. It almost comes down to a gut feeling, an intuitive sense that the time has come to finally make a decision. Debates usually resolve themselves, though. Typically, after a few days, people run out of things to say on memo-list or others start saying, "Enough already!"

Even then, once there is a resolution, challenges arise that involve getting on board with support for that decision and implementing it even if people still personally disagree with it. In my early days at Red Hat, I struggled when I heard how people continued to voice their disagreement with a decision we made, even after many of us had already moved on. I still struggle with it. That kind of dynamic is unfathomable in a more conventional organization. Most people would rather say, "I'm on board" with the decision, even if they aren't. That doesn't happen at Red Hat—people tell you what they think—which can really cut in two directions when you're trying to get something accomplished.

When you add up challenges like these, you can see how difficult it is to not just throw up your hands occasionally and say, "Just do it. I am the CEO and I'm telling you that I want this order followed." Admittedly, this kind of thing still happens sometimes, especially with time-sensitive decisions involving regulations, budgets, or some such where we don't have time to let the debate flame out before we act. In 2008, as the Great Recession hit us, we needed to reduce budgets without soliciting much input on how to do it. But when this does happen, most of our leaders do a pretty good job of saying, "I hear what you're saying, and I agree, that aspect isn't ideal. But for Red Hat right now, these other factors are outweighing that issue, and although I know this isn't the direction you want us to go in, it is what we're going to do. And you might be right—I might be making a mistake here—but I'm the one who needs to make this call, and if I'm wrong, we'll circle back and figure out how to correct it."

We also understand that whenever we operate outside the lines in this way, it damages our culture by some degree. It's like walking through a bed of perennial flowers: you don't always know what kind of subtle damage or change you can bring about with just a single footstep. So while it might seem as if you're opening yourself up to more problems by working inclusively, at Red Hat, we truly believe the benefits of facing challenges like these far outweigh the costs. It's a balancing act that requires constant care and attention.

It remains important for us to embrace the notion of "on our best day," where we strive to operate on the key principles we espouse in running an open organization, while also knowing we aren't perfect. We will stumble from time to time. But, in the end, Red Hat is a stronger organization as a result.

Jim's Leadership Tips

1. *Find or create a venue in which to discuss areas where you would like to see your team make progress.*

2. *Tell your team members about a problem you are trying to solve.* See how they respond, and if they are able to help solve it.

3. *In an area where you would like to see progress, ask questions of your team rather than request action.* Most likely, action will occur.

4. *Create some space for your team to innovate by purposely leaving some ambiguity in your direction on a specific process or task.*

5. *Ask your team to come to you with ideas and proposals.* Engage and discuss them, regardless of whether you move forward with them.

EPILOGUE

It's a Journey

As CEO of a public company, I'm a practitioner, not an academic. I don't pretend to have developed a new management system, though I hope I have described why a new one is needed. The only proof I can offer that the leadership culture we've built at Red Hat is effective and worth emulating—regardless of what kind of company you run—is our results. But I also admit that since Red Hat operates on the bleeding edge of this new and better way to lead, we cut ourselves quite often as well.

In short, we're still on a journey to find newer and better ways to build on the lessons we've learned about what works, and what doesn't, in building and leading participative communities.

The Boundaries of Participative Organizations

We know participative communities can build software. We see participative communities like Silicon Valley yield tremendous innovation, and efforts like Wikipedia can collect vast amounts of disparate information. Few would doubt the power of crowdsourcing to drive unique and elegant solutions to specific problems. Conversely, it's generally accepted that conventional hierarchies are typically miserable at driving innovation or sparking creativity. But those same hierarchies do excel at maintaining control and coordinating disparate activities like those involved in building complex machinery. Can participative organizations excel in these areas too? Put simply, could a loosely organized participative community build something as complicated as a jetliner?

This question first arose in a conversation I had with Gary Hamel, who was one of the first people to recognize the need for an entirely new management system to meet the needs of the twenty-first century. We were discussing the power of participation as a management model. While we both agree that this new system offers great potential in unlocking creativity and innovation, we were debating whether it could match and replace conventional management for purposes of coordination and, if so, what its limits might be. We ended up using the analogy of building a jetliner as our best example of a situation in which very tight coordination across literally millions of various systems and parts—the hallmark of a hierarchical system—is required. That question has been nagging me ever since.

Airplanes are truly modern marvels of coordination on a massive scale. A well-designed airplane is the result of tens of thousands of small design trade-offs that are perfectly balanced and tightly managed. Hundreds of thousands of components must come together with minute tolerances. A slight change to the wing design, intended to reduce wind drag just a bit, might require hundreds of additional changes, from the avionics to the landing gear. Every design choice and change must be analyzed across the many thousands of interconnected components. The end product is an engineering marvel of startling reliability. Indeed, the design and manufacture of an airplane represents the pinnacle of what modern coordination can produce.

Which brings me back to the question, can a bottom-up, participative system develop something as complex as a jetliner, considering the requirement for such close coordination among the various parts? When Hamel originally posed this question to me, my knee-jerk answer was no. Building a plane is not what participative systems are good at. Upon further reflection, I would more clearly say, "In the very short term and in the strictest sense of the question, my answer is no." While participative communities have shown an amazing ability to develop highly complex systems, their power lies in the distributed nature of the innovation process.

Think about how Linux is created. Those closest to individual components are able to drive optimized solutions to those problems. In these self-emergent systems, the underlying detail and complexity of the components can be far beyond anything a top-down, centrally planned system can muster. However, if those components must be tightly coordinated to work together, I'm not sure participative systems have a way to do that.

But the more I thought about the problem, the more I realized that *it's the wrong question*. It is asking whether a participative system stuck into the middle of a conventional command-and-control ecosystem can outperform it. The right question to ask is, "Could an open ecosystem in aviation produce a superior aircraft over time?" And to that question, my answer is yes.

The power of participative systems and bottom-up innovation comes from having those closest to the problems involved in solving them. Linux is successful not because Linus Torvalds specified his requirements for each component, but rather because he did not. He allowed others with different skills and expertise to drive the various components of the system, and ultimately the whole has benefited. If the various parties involved in the myriad components of aviation—from the electronic navigation system to the landing gear—were allowed to drive their own designs forward, would the benefits of the superior individual components offset the fact that they are not as tightly optimized to work together?

For many years, tightly coupled RISC/Unix systems represented the ultimate in computing performance. The idea was that, by producing both the hardware and the software together, a vendor could produce the fastest computers. These systems dominated high-end computing for years. Today, however, Red Hat Enterprise Linux, which is not designed for any particular hardware platform, runs over half the world's equity trading volume—and those are systems bought for performance, not price. Why?

Simply, no single engineered process can keep up with the pace of change capable in an open system, which can innovate faster because it is not encumbered with the need to coordinate across an entire system. Intel can run at its own pace, delivering the promise of Moore's Law with chips of ever-growing complexity and performance. It can do this without worrying about the software. Others are working globally to ensure the software continues to get faster and more reliable. The fact that virtually all the top supercomputers worldwide are running a combination of Intel chips and Linux demonstrates the power of allowing specialized groups to focus on optimizing in their own sphere to create a better whole. An open system could not create the tightly coupled, highly coordinated system that is a RISC/Unix computer. Instead, it created something better, faster, and cheaper.

But it did not happen overnight. A perennial garden takes years to reach maturity; the same can be said for a participative ecosystem. It took over a decade for the combination of x86 chips and Linux to surpass the power of tightly coordinated engineered systems. There are already open source projects trying to build an airplane. They are starting small, but who knows where they may be in a decade.

I'm not yet advocating the complete demolition of the conventional organizational structure. At Red Hat, we continue to experiment with the boundaries of applying this new model to a public company. We use our participative culture to drive innovation and make decisions quickly, and we still have people managers and senior leaders who play critical roles in catalyzing the company's direction, fostering participation, and driving its purpose and passion.

We are on a journey. I doubt anyone at Intel in the early days of the microprocessor would have imagined that its chips would run the world's fastest computers. Nor did Linus Torvalds ever dream of the same. I firmly believe we are on a path toward a new, superior management paradigm. Red Hat is one of the companies on the bleeding edge of that journey, and I hope our lessons learned—both positive and negative—about driving the principles of an open organization can help to catalyze the discussion.

A Shared Challenge

A key takeaway from this book is the notion that the Red Hat system— the way we go about getting work done—is a crucial source of our competitive advantage. Our management system and organizational culture generate unique capabilities that others simply cannot duplicate. In other words, our open organization is our competitive advantage. It's how we have fended off much bigger rivals in the past and how we plan to defend against them into the future.

Capabilities like speed and agility, rather than physical assets, will become even more important components of every company's competitive advantage in the future. But to capitalize on that advantage, you'll need an open organization management system capable of fueling those fires. We at Red Hat beat our competitors to market and react more quickly to threats and opportunities not because we pedal faster, but because the organization taps into powerful energy sources like purpose, passion, and community that make it move faster.

It would have been easy for me to rely exclusively on examples from Red Hat for this book. However, I purposely included a number of examples from Delta and other organizations like Whole Foods, W. L. Gore, and Zappos to demonstrate that any kind of organization can benefit from these principles. Many conventional competitors will face an onslaught of new entrants into their markets; just look at how Amazon continues to expand into retail or how Airbnb has disrupted the hospitality industry. These new players are likely to have a different, more modern organizational model driving their success. Competing against them isn't just about matching up your products in a market-based chess game. It's more about pitting organizational capabilities against each other. I hope this idea serves as food for thought for executives at both emerging businesses and established ones. To leaders at emerging companies, please don't assume that getting big means getting rigid and bureaucratic. To leaders in established companies, recognize that your organization's capabilities may become more important than your physical assets.

There's No Going Back

I have had the unique privilege to observe and learn this new management system up close. When I first joined Red Hat, I had my "conventional organization" filter on. I thought what I was seeing was simply chaos—the result of not adopting the tried-and-true management practices used universally by conventional organizations. Over time, however, I began to appreciate the subtleties of what I now realize is a different management paradigm. I've had a chance to poke and prod and experiment. I've seen how the principles we rely on at Red Hat operate in the extreme within open source communities like Linux. There is still much to learn, and I am sure there is much to tweak in terms of perfecting how open organizations operate. But there is one certainty in my mind: I could never go back.

Every leader who takes on a new job must undergo his or her own personal journey. I have had the unique opportunity to join a company that was already practicing the principles of open organization. That's been transformative for how I think about what makes companies successful. Every company must have a higher purpose, for example, and an enterprise can only exist and be profitable if it is creating value for someone. An organization's leaders have the job of sharpening and clarifying that purpose in a way that ignites the passion of its members.

To fulfill that role, I've learned that the leaders of tomorrow must possess traits that have largely been overlooked in conventional organizations. To effectively lead an open organization, a leader must possess the following traits:

> *Personal strength and confidence.* Leaders in the conventional world leverage their positional power—their titles—to get things done. But when working in a meritocracy, leaders need to earn respect. They can only do that if they have the confidence to admit they don't have all the answers. They must have a willingness to talk through problems and think on their feet in order to reach the best conclusions with the help of their teams.

Patience. The media rarely tell stories about how "patient" a leader is. But they should. When you are working to get the best effort and results from your team, to engage in dialogue for hours on end, and to do things again and again until they're done right, you need to have patience.

High "EQ." Too often we tout the intellectual capabilities of leaders by focusing on their IQ, when we should really be valuing their emotional intelligence quotient or EQ score. Being the smartest person in the room is not enough if you don't have the capacity to work with the people who are in that room with you. When you work with and through communities of contributors as Red Hat does, where you can't order anyone to do anything for you, your ability to listen, process, and not take everything personally becomes incredibly valuable.

A different mind-set. Leaders who have come up through conventional organizations have been indoctrinated in a quid pro quo mind-set—one that's been influenced by math and hard science that says every action should receive an appropriate response. But when you take a longer-term outlook to investing in something like building a community, you need to think differently. It's like trying to build a delicately balanced ecosystem in which any misstep you make can create imbalance and lead to long-term damage that you may not see right away. Leaders must divest themselves of the mind-set that requires them to achieve results today at all costs to one in which the big payoffs come from delaying their sense of gratification and making those investments in the future.

Of course, making these kinds of changes won't appeal to everyone. There are times when issuing a top-down edict, for instance, would be far easier than allowing the meritocracy to reach a solution on its own time. Why would you want to open yourself up to criticism from your own troops? Wouldn't your workplace seem less chaotic and in control if you stuck with doing the things the way you always have? To make this kind of culture work requires that leaders make an enormous investment in terms of time and energy, which can seem both daunting and wasteful. It's almost like taking a leap of faith into the unknown. How will you know that you and your organization will be able to reap positive rewards by going down the path I've described?

The answer comes back to the kind of competitive environment your organization faces. If you feel extreme pressure to keep up with the rapid pace of your market and competitors, as we do at Red Hat, then I believe the investments you make toward building an open organization will be paid back in spades. Once you see the power of unlocking the full potential of the people you work with, you simply can't imagine going back. I am gratified to be part of a system that helps enable people to achieve their potential. It's fun and exciting. Passion is contagious. I work to kindle it, but I am also consumed by the passion of others.

Another key lesson of this book is that the sense of pride I feel in what Red Hat has accomplished actually has little to do with anything I have personally accomplished. Rather, I feel proud for what the people of Red Hat have done as a direct result of my support for the system that enables them to achieve great things. This feeling is similar to how most people feel when their child graduates from college; they feel prouder than they ever felt about their own graduation. There is just something about seeing someone you care about and support step up and take the initiative to achieve something remarkable that is very powerful and, ultimately, gratifying. Watching the people around you blossom and reach their potential is so potent. When you allow everyone to do his or her best, and are wise enough not to stick yourself in the middle and muck things up, everybody wins.

This journey has been extraordinary for me. I've written this book about how the new type of organization, the open organization, is more effective and more capable. It's also a story about my own deeply satisfying and gratifying experience in learning how to lead such a workforce—something I couldn't have done without the help and feedback from everyone who works at Red Hat. Starting with my first interview up to today's billion-dollar company, it's been quite a ride—one I am thrilled to continue into the future. When I add everything up, it's easy for me to reflect on the true pleasure of working at Red Hat.

Join Us on Our Journey

Great conversations are happening on opensource.com, the website we created to spark discussions about what is possible when you open yourself to the possibilities of working in an open source way.

There is a case study on the site that specifically discusses how people are building their versions of "makerplanes" by tapping into the collective wisdom and expertise of the community. No, they aren't making jetliners . . . yet. But I wouldn't bet against them. This then raises the question, what else is possible when we put aside our conventional organizations and begin to tap into the power of participative communities in all aspects of our lives and businesses? The potential is limitless, which is why I invite you to join us on our journey by engaging in the discussions on opensource.com.

Epilogue

There is a special page related to the themes of this book, and we encourage you, in the spirit of letting the sparks fly, to share your thoughts and opinions with us on how you think we can all lead and work better in the future. We look forward to hearing from you there.

How Does Red Hat Make Billions of Dollars Selling Free Software?

People frequently ask me, "How does Red Hat make money selling free software?" This question comes up so often that I can't imagine not addressing it in this book, even if it's in an appendix. Let's start with an analogy: why do people choose to buy a bottle of water, when the same substance is freely available in most of the world? All you need to do is open a tap to get it, just as you can go online and download, say, open source software code. Yet many people find good reasons to pay several dollars for that bottle of water or sign up for a delivery service: the convenience and portability of the bottle, the perceived safety of the water's source, or even because people prefer the taste compared to tap water. The buying decision comes down to choice and whether the vendor is providing something of value to you.

Similarly, although it might appear that Red Hat's business model is to sell something that is supposed to be free, our company actually is in the business of adding value to free code. Red Hat is an ever-growing collaboration of both internal and external communities of contributors who update and improve software by working together. While Red Hat first made its name in the software world by working with the Linux operating system, which may be the most widely used software technology in the entire computer industry, we now collaborate with a multitude of other open source communities such as OpenStack, JBoss, GlusterFS, and Apache Camel in ways that provide value for our customers.

For our flagship product, Red Hat Enterprise Linux, for instance, we take the latest version of Linux and dissect it so that we can test and document every modification or bug-fix that has occurred since the last release. We certify it against the thousands of hardware and software programs that enterprises typically use, so they can confidently implement Red Hat Enterprise Linux without worrying about if or how it will work with the myriad other components of their data center. In addition, we have a dedicated security response team to identify, patch, and distribute fixes for malware. Unfortunately, the internet is making the "pipes and sewers" of computing as risky as drinking from a pool of water in the middle of a swamp. Our "bottled open source" solutions provide security that simply cannot be achieved otherwise. In short, we sell our customers peace of mind that their entire system is the most stable and secure system possible on the planet. That's something they're willing to pay us for.

Learning from Linux

We alone don't do all the work that our customers benefit from. We work as part of an open source community, which is much more powerful at delivering results than any one single siloed organization can.

Consider how the dynamics of the Linux community, of which Red Hat is part, operates. Created by Linus Torvalds in 1991 (he famously kicked off with a listserv note that read: "Hello everybody out there . . . I'm doing a [free] operating system . . . just a hobby, nothing professional . . ."), Linux now runs everything from the most extreme scientific computers to web servers, network devices, point of sale systems, military systems, cameras, automobiles, and mobile devices. If you're using an Android phone, you're using Linux.

The Linux story is fascinating from an organizational management perspective precisely because it involves a system in which literally thousands of people, including many Red Hatters, self-organize and take direction from informal leaders who emerge based on the quality of contributions they have made over time—which some community members have come to refer to as a "mega-self-organizing collective." The Linux source code itself, some 30 million lines of programming instructions, is accessible to just about everyone out there; hence, the term "open source." To create this code, community members came together in a decentralized manner, rather than working through a conventional top-down hierarchy, where higher-ups issued orders that were fulfilled by programmers at the lower rungs.

I am constantly amazed at the effectiveness of this self-organizing, opt-in, global community that we contribute to. This virtual army fixes bugs, heads off malevolent hackers, and collaborates on making Linux a stronger product than it would be if just a single entity tried to control it, which many people once thought was the only way to build software. Linux is modular enough to run things as diverse as refrigerators to smart phones to mainframe computers. It's precise enough to run some of the most mission-critical systems in the world, including stock exchanges and nuclear submarines. And it's scalable enough to run Google's infrastructure. The Linux community also reacts at amazing speed. Everything from security issues, when they arise, to breakthrough enhancements are typically addressed within hours or minutes.

For example, the US Navy, one of our customers, came to us with a major problem. Events in recent conflicts had proven that smaller boats armed with missiles posed a serious threat to the larger ships like aircraft carriers. The navy wanted to develop antimissile systems that could react in real time to those kinds of threats. The problem is that most operating systems don't work in real time. Think about the last time you were typing a document or working on a spreadsheet and your computer paused or experienced some kind of delay. That was because your operating system was working on other things in the background. While that's fine for most of us, the navy clearly needed something better.

But rather than trying to come up with its own solution, the navy came to Red Hat and the Linux community for help in building a "real-time kernel" that wouldn't experience those kinds of delays. We then helped catalyze the various Linux communities to tackle the project as something that everyone could benefit from. What happened over the next eighteen months was that the community worked together to create what the navy needed. But that same technology now used to help shoot down missiles is also used by stock exchanges to help ensure there is never any lag during the trading day. That's because our community includes members from organizations like JPMorgan Chase and Goldman Sachs, which saw the value in this effort, and led to a way to solve their problems. In other words, an open source community like Linux works because its members both directly and indirectly benefit from the work that they contribute.

People invest their time in making Linux a better operating system because, by virtue of making computing safer, faster, and more open, they feel as if they make the world a better place. It's that compelling purpose that brings so many people together to work on Linux and other open source projects. Not just programmers, but also writers, testers, marketers, designers, and administrators contribute their combined efforts to create something no one traditional organization could do on its own. One study estimated, for instance, that if you started from scratch, it would take about eight thousand years of development time to recreate Linux, at a reported cost of more than $10 billion.[1] That's powerful stuff.

Harnessing the Power of Community

The Linux story helps explain why we at Red Hat have come to appreciate that the open source development model is incredibly powerful at delivering innovation at a faster and less costly rate than the traditional software development model. And as Linux has evolved, so, too, has Red Hat.

In 1998, Red Hat had seventy-five associates and was earning $10 million in yearly sales, mostly from shipping Linux on CD-ROMs and selling T-shirts. People paid Red Hat for a version of Linux so they could get access to documentation and support. While Red Hat experienced a highly successful initial public offering in August 1999 using that business model, the dot-com crash almost brought the company down with it. The company's stock, which traded as high as $286 a share in December 1999 (leading to an eye-popping valuation of about $19.7 billion), had cratered to about $3.50 by 2001 as the company continued to hemorrhage cash and struggled to grow revenue. That meant that if Red Hat was going to survive, it needed to evolve its business model to become profitable—fast. That was especially true because Red Hat competed against some of the mightiest tech companies around, a few of whom were extremely vocal in their derision of a business model they called "communist." As Bill Gates, former CEO of Microsoft, told the press back in 2001, "We think of Linux as a competitor in the student and hobbyist market but I really don't think in the commercial market we'll see it in any significant way."[2]

Unlike other business stories, which involve heroic CEOs riding to the rescue, Red Hat's turnaround came from within. A collection of engineers, businesspeople, and lawyers identified as "the smartest people in the company," according to Mike Evans, Red Hat's vice president of business development, helped the fledgling company pivot its early business model. After debating several options, including some that would make Red Hat's software proprietary, the team came up with the idea to completely shift focus from the desktop to the enterprise server—a key turning point in Red Hat history, though not a popular decision at the time. In fact, Paul Cormier (now Red Hat's president of products and technologies), a key architect of the now powerful "enterprise open source" business model, received a "does not meet expectations" for his performance review in the year that he developed the business model. (He's obviously more than met expectations in the subsequent decade.)

But when Red Hat shifted its focus to the enterprise IT market, it dawned on folks like Cormier that as powerful as open source is at solving problems, it can also create quite a few issues for companies as well. For example, open source development breaks down problems into smaller chunks that groups work on, which results in the frequent and early release of software that can be problematic for companies needing stability perhaps more than rapid change. And unlike traditional software with long release cycles, developers don't fix bugs in older versions of code. They simply fix those problems in their next release, which again creates issues that affect applications for many years. The fast-moving, modular approach to writing software has many advantages over the traditional software development model, but it does not make it easy to use for running large, mission-critical applications liking billing systems or trading platforms that require absolute stability and as little change as possible.

If you're running, say, a stock exchange, you need to know that any updates to your software won't crash the entire system. Or, if you run several kinds of hardware in your business, you need to know for certain that the latest software update will run equally well on all of your machines or it simply won't be valuable to your business. Red Hat steps in to stabilize the software while providing support and documentation. When we "freeze the spec," as it's called, Red Hat is actually making a significant investment in that we dedicate several hundred engineers to supporting each version of Linux for the next ten years. As changes occur upstream in the Linux community, our team will be working to create patches to the older versions of the code that our customers are running in a way that keeps their business running smoothly. Put another way, we generate our revenues by making open source software consumable, and safe, for enterprises to adopt.

By investing in tech labs of our own, not to mention the kind of top talent needed to run that kind of support backbone, Red Hat is able to provide value to our customers through services they pay for on a subscription basis. One of the real values that Red Hat delivers through its subscription model is that we don't have any built-in incentives to deliver software to our customers that they don't want or need. When you buy a Red Hat product, you are buying the support and value-added infrastructure for whatever product you buy without any hidden incentives to add new code and features—known as software bloat—that you didn't ask for.

In short, by providing these services to our customers, and actively contributing and giving back to the open source communities that make everything possible, we're able to make billions of dollars selling free software. We're proud of that because we feel that our customers are receiving an incredible value compared to proprietary alternatives. Since the code itself is free, our customers pay only for the added value we provide. That means that customers not only reap the benefits of the innovative capabilities of the code created by open source communities, but also get the stability and security they need, all for about one-tenth the price of what our competitors offer. That's why it's easy to see that the future of software is all about the open source way.

NOTES

Chapter 1

1. Chris Grams, "Tom Sawyer, whitewashing fences, and building communities online," OpenSource.com, September 9, 2009, https://opensource .com/business/09/9/tom-sawyer-whitewashing-fences-and-building-communities-online.

2. Jim Collins and Jerry Porras, *Built to Last* (New York: HarperBusiness, 1995), 9.

3. "The World's Most Innovative Companies," Forbes.com, http://www .forbes.com/innovative-companies/list/; Megan Rose Dickey, "The 25 Best Tech Companies To Work For In 2013," *Business Insider,* July 12, 2013, http://www.businessinsider.com/top-25-tech-companies-to-work-at-in-2013-2013-7?op=1#ixzz3Kmmp9qyH.

4. To learn more about the Red Hat business model, see the appendix.

Chapter 2

1. John Mackey and Raj Sisodia, *Conscious Capitalism* (Boston: Harvard Business Review Press, 2013), 33–34.

2. Linda Hill, Greg Brandeau, Emily Truelove, and Kent Lineback, *Collective Genius* (Boston: Harvard Business Review Press, 2014), 92.

3. Michael Burchell and Jennifer Robin, *The Great Workplace: How to Build It, How to Keep It, and Why It Matters* (San Francisco: Jossey-Bass, 2011), 133.

4. Hill et al., *Collective Genius,* 46–47.

5. Ibid., 55.

6. Ibid., 92.

7. Gary Hamel, "The Problem With Management," *The Guardian,* March 9, 2012.

8. Mig Pascual, "Zappos: 5 Out-of-the-Box Ideas for Keeping Employees Engaged," *U.S. News & World Report*, October 30, 2012.

9. Mackey and Sisodia, *Conscious Capitalism*, 183–184.

10. "Why These 6 Companies Are the Best Places to Work in Medical Sales," *Business Insider*, January 20, 2014.

11. Burchell and Robin, *The Great Workplace*, 134.

12. Simon Sinek, "How Great Leaders Inspire Action" filmed September 2009. TED.com, http://www.ted.com/talks/simon_sinek_how_great_leaders_inspire_action?quote=709.

13. Burchell and Robin, *The Great Workplace*, 153.

14. Pascual, "Zappos."

Chapter 3

1. "Worldwide, 13% of Employees Are Engaged at Work," Gallup World, October 8, 2013, http://www.gallup.com/poll/165269/worldwide-employees-engaged-work.aspx.

2. Charles A. O'Reilly and Jeffrey Pfeffer, *Hidden Value: How Great Companies Achieve Extraordinary Results with Ordinary People* (Boston: Harvard Business School Press, 2000).

3. Burchell and Robin, *The Great Workplace*, 127.

4. It's worth noting that this measurement can be challenging because Red Hatters recognize that our culture isn't right for everyone, so many are inclined to say, "Yes, but it's not right for everyone" or "Yes, for the right person."

5. Mackey and Sisodia, *Conscious Capitalism*, 240.

6. Ibid., 241.

7. Burchell and Robin, *The Great Workplace*, 211.

8. Ibid., 46.

9. 2013 Forum Global Leadership Survey, December 20, 2013, http://www.slideshare.net/ForumCorp/forum-leadership-pulse-survey-2013-findings-implications.

10. Ibid.

11. Jack Stack with Bo Burlingham, *The Great Game of Business* (New York: Crown Business, 2013), 178.

Chapter 4

1. Brook Manville and Josiah Ober, *A Company of Citizens* (Boston: Harvard Business School Press, 2003), 10.

2. Ibid., 135–136.

3. Burchell and Robin, *The Great Workplace*, 43.

4. *Wikipedia*, s.v. "Meritocracy," last modified December 18, 2014, http://en.wikipedia.org/wiki/Meritocracy.

5. Liz Elting, "How I Grew: Meritocracy Helped Us Grow to a $350 Million Company," Translations.com, http://www.translations.com/about/news/in-the-news/how-i-grew-meritocracy-helped-us-grow-350-million-company.

6. Rajendra Sisodia, Jagdish N. Sheth, and David Wolfe, *Firms of Endearment* (Upper Saddle River, NJ: Pearson Education, 2014), 247.

7. Gary Hamel, "Innovation Democracy: W. L. Gore's Original Management Model," *Management Exchange*, September 23, 2010, http://www.managementexchange.com/story/innovation-democracy-wl-gores-original-management-model.

8. Rebecca Fernandez, "Building a positive meritocracy: It's harder than it sounds," OpenSource.com, August 25, 2010, http://opensource.com/business/10/8/building-positive-meritocracy-its-harder-it-sounds.

9. Alice Truong, "Why Google Axed Its '20% Time' Policy," *Fast Company*, August 16, 2013, http://www.fastcompany.com/3015877/fast-feed/why-google-axed-its-20-policy.

10. Burchell and Robin, *The Great Workplace*, 153–154.

11. Hamel, "Innovation Democracy."

12. Burchell and Robin, *The Great Workplace*, 41.

Chapter 5

1. Peter F. Drucker, "Managing Oneself," *Harvard Business Review*, January 2005, http://hbr.org/2005/01/managing-oneself/ar/1.

2. Jonah Lehrer, "Groupthink: The Brainstorming Myth," *The New Yorker*, January 30, 2012.

3. Richard Wiseman, *59 Seconds: Think a Little, Change a Lot* (New York: Random House, 2010), 213–214.

4. James Surowiecki, *The Wisdom of Crowds* (New York: Anchor, 2005), 36.

5. Hill et al., *Collective Genius*, 121.

6. Ed Catmull and Amy Wallace, *Creativity, Inc.* (New York: Random House, 2014), Kindle version, location 1374.

7. Hill et al., *Collective Genius*, 139.

8. Ibid., 24.

9. Linux Kernel Mailing List, https://lkml.org/lkml/2013/2/21/225.

10. Michael Hickins, "Linux Throw-Down Sheds Light on 'Moronic' Software Processes," *Wall Street Journal*, March 1, 2013.

11. Ibid.

12. Burchell and Robin, *The Great Workplace*, 27.

13. Ibid., 76.

14. Mackey and Sisodia, *Conscious Capitalism*, 261.

15. Catmull and Wallace, *Creativity, Inc.*

Chapter 6

1. "IBM Global Study: Majority of Organizational Change Projects Fail," IBM, October 14, 2008, http://www-03.ibm.com/press/us/en/pressrelease/25492.wss.

2. "New Standish Group Report Shows More Projects Are Successful and Less Projects Failing," Standish Group, 2011 CHAOS Report, March 3, 2011. http://www.marketwired.com/press-release/new-standish-group-report-shows-more-projects-are-successful-less-projects-failing-1405513.htm.

3. Burchell and Robin, *The Great Workplace*, 74.

4. Sisodia et al., *Firms of Endearment*, 230.

5. Adam Bryant, "What Eisenhower Taught Me About Decision-Making," *New York Times*, May 25, 2013, http://www.nytimes.com/2013/05/26/business/bill-marriott-jr-on-inclusive-decision-making.html?_r=0.

6. Tim Elkins, phone interview with author, September 9, 2014.

7. Hill et al., *Collective Genius*, 40.

8. PricewaterhouseCoopers, "Boosting Business Performance through Programme and Project Management," 2004, http://www.pwc.com/us/en/operations-management/assets/pwc-global-project-management-survey-first-survey-2004.pdf.

9. Kenneth R. Thompson, Ramon L. Benedetto, and Thomas J. Walter, *It's My Company Too!* (Austin, TX: Greenleaf Book Group Press, 2013), 26.

10. Sisodia et al., *Firms of Endearment*, 126.

Chapter 7

1. Shaun Abrahamson, Peter Ryder, and Bastian Unterberg, *Crowdstorm* (Hoboken, NJ: John Wiley & Sons, 2013), 166–167.

2. Beth Kowitt, "Whole Foods takes over America," *Fortune*, April 10, 2014, http://fortune.com/2014/04/10/whole-foods-takes-over-america/.

3. Mackey and Sisodia, *Conscious Capitalism*, 239.

4. Stephen Bernhut, "Primal Leadership, with Daniel Goleman," *Ivey Business Journal* 66, no. 5 (2002): 14–15.

Notes

5. The Economist Intelligence Unit, "The Rise of the Customer-led Economy," 2013, http://www.economistinsights.com/sites/default/files/EIU_Salesforce_Proof-7.pdf.

6. Gary Hamel, "Innovation Democracy."

7. Ibid.

8. Clay Shirky, *Here Comes Everybody* (New York: Penguin, 2008), 258–259.

9. Scott Cook, "Leadership in an Agile Age," (lecture at Innovation 2011: Entrepreneurship for a Disruptive World Conference, March 2011), http://network.intuit.com/2011/04/20/leadership-in-the-agile-age/.

10. Russ Arensman, "Cultivating Success," EDN Network, April 1, 2002: http://www.edn.com/electronics-news/4347919/Cultivating-Success.

Appendix

1. Amanda McPherson, Brian Proffitt, and Ron Hale-Evans, "Estimating the Total Development Cost of a Linux Distribution," The Linux Foundation, http://www.linuxfoundation.org/sites/main/files/publications/estimatinglinux.html.

2. Paul Thurrott, "Gates: Linux is no threat to Windows," Windows IT Pro, March 23, 1999, http://windowsitpro.com/windows-server/gates-linux-no-threat-windows.

BIBLIOGRAPHY

Abrahamson, Shaun, Peter Ryder, and Bastian Unterberg. *Crowdstorm.* Hoboken, NJ: John Wiley & Sons, 2013.

Ackof, Russell L. *The Democratic Corporation.* New York: Oxford University Press, 1994.

Burchell, Michael, and Jennifer Robin. *The Great Workplace: How to Build It, How to Keep It, and Why It Matters.* San Francisco: Jossey-Bass, 2011.

Catmull, Ed, and Amy Wallace. *Creativity, Inc.* New York: Random House, 2014.

Chesbrough, Henry. *Open Business Models.* Boston: Harvard Business School Press, 2006.

———. *Open Innovation.* Boston: Harvard Business School Press, 2003.

Hamel, Gary. *The Future of Management.* Boston: Harvard Business School Press, 2007.

Hill, Linda, Greg Brandeau, Emily Truelove, and Kent Lineback. *Collective Genius.* Boston: Harvard Business Review Press, 2014.

Hoffman, Reid, Ben Casnocha, and Chris Yeh. *The Alliance.* Boston: Harvard Business Review Press, 2014.

Howe, Jeff. *Crowdsourcing.* New York: Three Rivers Press, 2008.

Johnson, Steven. *Future Perfect.* New York: Penguin, 2012.

Mackey, John, and Raj Sisodia. *Conscious Capitalism.* Boston: Harvard Business Review Press, 2013.

Manville, Brook, and Josiah Ober. *A Company of Citizens.* Boston: Harvard Business School Press, 2003.

O'Reilly, Charles A., and Jeffrey Pfeffer. *Hidden Value.* Boston: Harvard Business School Press, 2000.

Osborn, Alex F. *Your Creative Power.* New York: Charles Scribner's Sons, 1948.

Shirky, Clay. *Here Comes Everybody.* New York: Penguin, 2008.

Sinek, Simon. *Start with Why.* New York: Portfolio, 2009.

Sisodia, Rajendra S., Jagdish N. Sheth, and David Wolfe. *Firms of Endearment.* Upper Saddle River, NJ: Pearson Education, 2014.

Sloane, Paul, ed. *A Guide to Open Innovation and Crowdsourcing.* Philadelphia: Kogan Page Limited, 2011.

Stack, Jack, with Bo Burlingham. *The Great Game of Business.* New York: Crown Business, 2013.

Surowiecki, James. *The Wisdom of Crowds.* New York: Anchor, 2005.

Tapscott, Don, David Ticoll, and Alex Lowy. *Digital Capital.* Boston: Harvard Business School Press, 2000.

Tapscott, Don, and David Ticoll. *The Naked Corporation.* New York: Penguin, 2003.

Tapscott, Don, and Anthony D. Williams. *Wikinomics.* New York: Portfolio Penguin, 2008.

———. *Macrowikinomics.* New York: Portfolio Penguin, 2010.

Thompson, Kenneth R., Ramon L. Benedetto, and Thomas J. Walter. *It's My Company Too!* Austin, TX: Greenleaf Book Group Press, 2013.

Wacksman, Barry, and Chris Stutzman. *Connected By Design.* San Francisco: Jossey-Bass, 2014.

Wiseman, Richard. *59 Seconds: Think a Little, Change a Lot.* New York: Random House, 2010.

INDEX

Index

Index

ACKNOWLEDGMENTS

First of all, I want to thank the thousands of current and former Red Hatters who are responsible for building the thriving open source culture we have today. I wrote this book to describe the amazing management system that they, not I, have created at Red Hat. This book is a tribute to all of their hard work and risk taking in bucking the traditional rules of business and creating a new way to organize and get work done that I continue to learn and grow from every day.

I have also had the benefit of standing on the shoulders of giants. I have learned so much in following what Red Hat's founders, Bob Young and Marc Ewing, put in motion. That's also true of the leadership of Matthew Szulik, my predecessor, who drove the company forward and continued to scale our culture. I owe a deep debt of gratitude as well to my senior management team—Charlie Peters, executive vice president and CFO; DeLisa Alexander, executive vice president and chief people officer; Jackie Yeaney, executive vice president, strategy and corporate marketing; Michael Cunningham, executive vice president and general counsel; Arun Oberoi, executive vice president, global sales and services; and Paul Cormier, executive vice president and president, products and technologies—which has remained remarkably intact since the day I started. But that's not to diminish the great work done by Brian Stevens and Alex Pinchev in their time with Red Hat as well. Most of my team has been together at Red Hat for more than a decade, and they have been instrumental in shaping our company's strategy, business model, and culture.

Writing a book is truly a team effort. Many Red Hatters worked to make this book a reality. In particular, I want to thank Leigh Day, Stephanie Wonderlick, and Emily Stancil Martinez, who first had the idea for a book on Red Hat's unique model for getting things done. I also want to thank Rebecca Fernandez, Máirín Duffy, Thomas Cameron, Jeff Mackanic, Kim Jokisch, and Laura Hamlyn for their time, perspective, and keen memory of many great Red Hat stories. Without your support and encouragement, and in the case of Emily, continuous prodding, this book would literally never have been written. Much credit must go to my assistant Andrea Ferrara, who has been with me since my days at The Boston Consulting Group. Without her stern management of my calendar, this book would never have happened.

I want to thank Darren Dahl, who collaborated with me on this effort. He feels more and more like a Red Hatter every day and continuously pushed my own thinking and understanding of what makes Red Hat such a great place. It's been a great partnership, and I will miss the many hours we spent together crafting the stories and messages in this book. Thanks also to our agent, Esmond Harmsworth, who has one of the best names in the literary world, and Melinda Merino, our editor at Harvard Business Review Press, and the entire HBR team for believing in our message and helping us share it with the world.

I would like to thank Gary Hamel for his thought leadership on this topic. His book *The Future of Management* remains the best articulation of the need for a new management paradigm. He has been a great thought partner for me, and I also thank him for his excellent and provocative foreword to this book.

Acknowledgments

Most importantly, I'd like to thank my wife, Lauren, and our fantastic twins, Jack and Emma, for their support and understanding. Lauren has been my thought partner not only for this book, but in all aspects of my business career and life for more than two decades. I would not be where I am without her. I especially thank my family for understanding when, even after I've been away on a long business trip overseas, I've had to lock myself away with the computer to work on the words within these pages. And finally my mother, who may have been my harshest copy editor, but also the person who has enabled all of my successes in life.

It's truly been a team effort, and this book, like the work we do every day, was the product of an open and collaborative effort that is far stronger than anything I could have done on my own.

ABOUT THE AUTHOR

JIM WHITEHURST is president and chief executive officer of Red Hat, the world's leading provider of open source enterprise IT products and services. With a background in business development, finance, and global operations, Whitehurst has proven expertise in helping companies flourish—even in the most challenging economic and business environments. Since joining Red Hat in 2008, Whitehurst has grown the company, and its influence in a variety of industries, by reaching key milestones—the most notable in 2012 when Red Hat became the first $1 billion revenue open source software company.

Under Whitehurst's leadership, Red Hat has been recognized on *Forbes*'s "Fastest-Growing Technology Companies" list in 2011, ranked seventh on *Investor's Business Daily*'s "Top 10 New American Companies" list in 2011, and ranked on *Forbes*'s list of "The World's Most Innovative Companies" in 2012 and 2014. Red Hat was selected for inclusion in the Standard & Poor's (S&P) 500 stock index in 2009, and named by Glassdoor in 2014 as one of the best places to work.

Red Hat's product portfolio has expanded through several strategic acquisitions since Whitehurst joined the company, including Qumranet, Inc. (virtualization), Makara (Platform-as-a-Service [PaaS]), Gluster (storage), FuseSource (middleware), Polymita (middleware), ManageIQ (cloud management), Inktank (storage), eNovance

(OpenStack), and FeedHenry (middleware). By incorporating these technologies, Red Hat has become the only open source company that can offer an open source cloud stack that includes an operating system, middleware, and virtualization. The company also revealed its open hybrid cloud technology vision for the future of IT, including plans for building and managing Infrastructure-as-a-Service (IaaS) and PaaS public and private clouds.

As its portfolio grows, Red Hat continues to influence the future of technology by supporting open source projects like OpenStack, Fedora, and GlusterFS, and by defending patent law legislation, including amicus submissions to the US Supreme Court. Open Source for America, a coalition advocating for open source software in government, also launched in 2009, with Red Hat as a founding member. In 2010, Red Hat unveiled opensource.com, a website that explores the role of open source in business, government, law, and life, and brings the open source message to a much broader audience.

Whitehurst continues to advocate for open, nonproprietary data and technology. He speaks at conferences throughout the world and at top research universities, including Harvard Business School, Duke University, and the University of North Carolina at Chapel Hill. Whitehurst is often asked to appear as a guest on CNBC, Bloomberg, and Fox Business.

Whitehurst began his career in 1989 at The Boston Consulting Group (BCG) in Chicago and held several corporate development leadership roles at the firm. Over the next decade, he worked in BCG's Chicago, Hong Kong, and Shanghai offices and as a partner in the Atlanta office, with numerous clients across a wide range of industries. He was named partner at BCG in 2000.

On September 11, 2001, the Delta Air Lines leadership team asked Whitehurst to serve as its acting treasurer. That same week, he led the company's secured debt offering, winning the Thomson-IVR "Deal of the Year" for reopening the capital markets. In 2002, he joined Delta Air Lines full-time as senior vice president–finance, treasury, and business development. He was promoted again in 2004 to chief network and planning officer, a position from which he drove significant international expansion. He was named chief operating officer in 2005, overseeing all aspects of airline operations, including sales, marketing, operations, and strategy.

Whitehurst graduated from Rice University in Houston, Texas, in 1989 with a bachelor of arts degree in economics and computer science. He also attended Fredrick Alexander University in Erlangen, Germany, and holds a general course degree from the London School of Economics. He earned his MBA from Harvard in 1994. In 2007, while COO of Delta Air Lines, Whitehurst was nominated as a Young Global Leader by the World Economic Forum. In March 2014, he was honored with the William C. Friday Award, an annual award presented by the senior class of Park Scholars, North Carolina State University's merit scholarship program, honoring Friday's dedication and excellence in leadership, scholarship, service, and character.

Whitehurst lives in Durham, North Carolina, with his wife and twins. He is a member of the board of directors of DigitalGlobe, Inc., Duke University Health System, and The Conservation Fund. He also sits on the executive committee of the North Carolina Chamber of Commerce.